Implementing

Implementing NCLB

*Creating a
Knowledge
Framework
to Support
School
Improvement*

Paul L. Kimmelman
Foreword by Denis P. Doyle

CORWIN PRESS
A SAGE Publications Company
Thousand Oaks, California

For information:

Corwin Press
A Sage Publications Company
2455 Teller Road
Thousand Oaks, California 91320
www.corwinpress.com

Sage Publications Ltd
1 Oliver's Yard
55 City Road
London EC1Y 1SP
United Kingdom

Sage Publications India Pvt. Ltd.
B-42, Panchsheel Enclave
Post Box 4109
New Delhi 110 017 India

Printed in the United States of America on acid-free paper

Library of Congress Cataloging-in-Publication Data

Kimmelman, Paul.
Implementing NCLB : creating a knowledge framework to support school improvement / Paul L. Kimmelman.
    p. cm.
Includes bibliographical references and index.
ISBN 1-4129-1713-1 (cloth) — ISBN 1-4129-1714-X (pbk.)
    1. United States. No Child Left Behind Act of 2001.
2. Educational accountability—United States. 3. School improvement programs—United States. I. Title.
LB2806.22.K56 2006
379.1'580973—dc22

                                            2005035811

05   06   07   08   10   9   8   7   6   5   4   3   2   1

Acquisitions editor:	Rachel Livsey
Editorial assistant:	Phyllis Cappello
Production editor:	Sanford Robinson
Copy editor:	Dan Hays
Typesetter:	C&M Digitals (P) Ltd.
Indexer:	Karen A. McKenzie
Cover Designer:	Rose Storey

Contents

Foreword   ix
  Denis P. Doyle

Preface   xvii

Acknowledgments   xxv

About the Author   xxvii

1. **Education Events That Led to NCLB**   1
   Activities and Reports   5
   Summary   23
   An Action Idea   24

2. **Using Knowledge to Build
   Organizational Capacity**   27
   What Is Knowledge?   31

3. **Knowledge Acquisition**   35
   Data Retreats   41
   Using Credible Research- or Evidence-Based
       Information or Both   48
   Setting a Context for Education Research:
       The National Research Council Committees   51
   U.S. Department of Education Research Initiative   52
   Using the Research Knowledge   56
   Summary   62
   Action Ideas for Knowledge Acquisition   63
   Other Research Organizations of Note   64

4. **Knowledge Management**   **67**
     Understanding Formative Assessment   73
     Examples of Knowledge Management Products   75
     Instructional Management Solutions   82
     Summary   88

5. **Knowledge Implementation**   **91**
     Knowledge Implementation Using
       Professional Development   98
     Study Groups   100
     Lesson Study   101
     Other Professional Development Activities   102
     Action Research   103
     Individually Guided Activities   104
     Teacher Leaders   104
     Lessons for Districtwide Reform Leadership   105
     Summary   106
     Action Idea From Dr. Ken Arndt   109

6. **Courageous School Leadership and
   the Challenge of NCLB**   **115**
     Creating a Challenge Mind-Set Using Stories   115
     The People and Their Stories   117
     A Hopeful Result of Building
       Organizational Capacity to Implement NCLB   119

7. **Final Words**   **125**
     The Knowledge Model   125
     Final Thoughts on NCLB   127

Resource A: Tibbott Case Study   **129**
     Building a Team: Shared Leadership Takes Hold   129
     Background   130
     Strengths Going Into the Partnership   133
     Challenges Going Into the Partnership   133
     Key Professional Development Activities
       and Events—Year 1 (2002–2003)   134
     Year 2 (2003–2004)   140
     The Current Picture (2004–2005)   143

Resource B: High School Reform   149
    U.S. Department of Education Research and Reports   151
    Policies and Practices   154
    Rigorous Research   161

References   163

Index   167

Foreword

Mend Not End

Who would have guessed 4 years ago—when the bloom was on the NCLB rose—that it would today need spirited defenders, people who see beyond the partisan rhetoric? As it turns out, because NCLB set its sights so high it now needs all the friends it can get—and not policy wonks but practitioners who know whereof they speak.

Yet the opposition NCLB has garnered is strange. Spell it out: NCLB, no child left behind. As an idea, it is beyond reproach: Who, indeed, should policy and practice leave behind? Your child? My child? Uncle Sam has overreached, opponents argue, forcing unfunded mandates on the states. If, as they aver, education is the state's business and not the federal government's, does that mean that they are prepared to defend the indefensible? Is it all right for states to leave the poor and dispossessed behind?

Is it all right, in the name of states rights, to leave racial minorities behind? Who should our schools be educating if not the least among us? True, there is no federal constitutional mandate for education. Indeed, the reserve powers clause of the Tenth Amendment actually reserves to the states any powers not specifically enumerated for the federal government. The constitutional mantle for education is state by state, not federal. Do these state constitutional mandates legitimize leaving the less fortunate behind?

Paul Kimmelman is just the person to offer a spirited defense of NCLB. A former school superintendent currently at Learning Point Associates in Illinois, he has been deeply involved in school improvement throughout his career. Indeed, Paul has served not just the districts in which he worked but also the nation as a whole, first as president of the First in the World Consortium, then as a member of the TIMSS-R Technical Review Panel, and recently as a member of the Glenn Commission (National Commission on Mathematics and Science Teaching). He has the grounding of a practitioner with the perspective of a policy maven. His view is simultaneously on the ground and at 30,000 feet.

Perhaps more to the point, Paul's defense of NCLB is not defensive but generous. A friendly critic, Paul first sets NCLB in its historical context. He argues that NCLB is not only conceptually correct but also worth reforming to smooth out the rough spots. That is tough love.

This, his latest book, is "an attempt to be a useful guide for understanding how NCLB became a law and, most important, building organizational capacity to implement school improvement to comply with it." He focuses on building organizational capacity to avoid repeating mistakes of the past and to help educators understand the process of reform "to prevent more policy mandates in the future." To do so, he encourages practitioners to "recognize the importance of acquiring, managing, and implementing knowledge to inform decision making."

This is a tall order, particularly when many educators are notoriously averse to data-driven decision making. In fairness, it must be said that there is a reason for this aversion; historically, education data were something a third party required you to gather (about yourself) to embarrass you with 90 to 120 days later—or so it seemed. When data are used diagnostically, however—and to celebrate success as well as pinpoint problems—it is no longer a game of gotcha. As Montgomery County, Maryland, Superintendent Jerry D. Weast notes, today he uses data to catch you doing something right. That, indeed, is the promise of systematic knowledge acquisition, management, and implementation. It is made possible by modern information technology, which puts data in the hands of users in real time.

* * * * *

As Paul points out, rarely does legislation see the light of day that is so widely praised for its intent: Who can argue with so noble a sentiment as to leave no child behind? Yet, as this book goes to print, the drums of NCLB war are beating. Among other critics, the National Education Association is suing, all the while saying precious little about the framers' noble intentions. Also, a small but increasing number of states are threatening to go their own way. Among the shrinking list of defenders of the federal role is the Education Trust, one of NCLB's most stalwart supporters. It at least is keeping faith.

In this connection, it is worth noting that NCLB is a direct outgrowth of half a century of federal concern about school improvement. Interestingly, the school improvement impulse—until the present day—was not rooted in pedagogical concerns but, rather, grew organically out of the commendable impulse to extend and defend the civil rights of the poor, dispossessed, and racially and ethnically different. Equity and access were the issues, and rightly so. They had been systematically denied and could be counted and weighed; there was no pretending otherwise. As so many of us thought at the time, performance would take care of itself.

Because the denial of access and equity was undemocratic in the extreme, the solution appeared to be straightforward: to achieve access, open doors; to achieve equity, spend more money. As Irving Kristol noted in another context, solving the problem of poverty among the elderly was simple: Give them money. This is precisely what happened and explains why poverty among the elderly declined so steeply in the late 20th century.

Education and civil rights, however, although natural collaborators, were a different matter. Not to put too fine a point on it, Lyndon B. Johnson's concurrent War on Poverty and Elementary and Secondary Education Act rested on a shared assumption that education was the way up and out. Establish access (open doors) and initiate equity (let money flow) and the poor and dispossessed would flock to education like bees to honey. Not only would they flock to education, mirabile dictu, education would work its magic. To those of us who shared this vision, the logic seemed impeccable: The poor had been denied. The end of denial would spell the end of poverty. Would that it had been so.

The bitter truth is that even with all the goodwill in the world, spontaneous transformation was not an option. Title 1, for example, between its inception and NCLB's enactment, spent $135 billion on the most commendable of objectives—to improve the academic performance (in reading and math) of low-income youngsters. Unfortunately, a third of a century later, there is precious little in the way of academic improvement to show for it.

Thus, the mantra, mend not end, speaks not just to fine-tuning NCLB but also to the federal role in education. Remember, it took a seismic shift in the body politic to launch a federal role at all: Russia's Sputnik did us all a favor by permitting Ike to mobilize a limited but significant foray into heretofore foreign territory. The National Defense Education Act was the federal government's maiden voyage into the uncharted seas of elementary and secondary education, even in a small way. (Twenty years later, it prompted Education Commissioner Ernie Boyer to wistfully wish that the Japanese would put a Toyota in orbit.)

The second and bigger seismic shift was the assassination of John F. Kennedy and the ascendancy of Lyndon B. Johnson, a larger-than-life wheeler-dealer with the most powerful connections and persuasive skills imaginable. In his first 100 days, Johnson was able to do what no predecessor could have even tried: He forged a sweeping federal role that is with us to this day. Indeed, so deeply embedded is it that it is difficult to even imagine that it was not always thus.

A third of a century is a long time, even by Washington standards, and it is clear that an active federal role is here to stay. Change it must, change it will, but it will not go away. The logic of demanding performance is irreproachable. As Humphrey Institute fellow and former Democratic state senator of Minnesota John Brandle states, "There will be more dollars for education when there is more education for the dollar."

* * * * *

Indeed, so interesting is the fallout from President Bush's approach to the federal role that it bears a quick reexamination. Not long ago, education was a Democratic exclusive. Republicans decried the imminent death of that most American of icons—local control. Remember, President Reagan, conservative icon personified, had proposed that Jimmy Carter's Department of Education be abolished (Reagan could not find a sponsor for the necessary legislation and the idea died aborning). It is also entertaining to remember that Reagan's budget proposed education cuts so severe that the congressional Democrats declared it dead on arrival; in turn, their largess was unparalleled, permitting Reagan (when he ran for a second term) to claim that his was the presidency that spent more on education than any in history. (As Henry Kissinger was reputed to have said, it has the added virtue of being true.)

For his part, Mr. Dole (running against Bill Clinton) attacked the teachers' unions and the federal role in education generally to the glee of Democrats. All the more surprising that the second President Bush would engulf education in a passionate embrace. Like Nixon's opening to China, it took a fundamental role reversal to adopt what had heretofore been the exclusive province of liberal Democrats.

Americans have been and will continue to be generous with education because they believe in it. Indeed, the two largest domestic programs ever enacted—larger even than social security, the transcontinental railroads, or the interstate highway system—were education programs: the land grant colleges of the mid-19th century and the GI Bill of the mid-20th century. Each symbolized its time and place: The land grant colleges (the Morrill Act) used physical capital to collateralize human capital, whereas the GI Bill went straight to the source, paying stipends to underwrite human capital formation. (In its initial incarnation, the GI Bill paid living expenses only, not tuition. The memory of McArthur pushing the Bonus Army out of Washington was still fresh, and the prospect of demobilizing 12 million veterans into a shaky economy was a daunting one.)

Indeed, so popular was the GI Bill and so widely admired was it that it has not attracted much in the way of critical scholarship. It worked, and it worked wonderfully well. As a consequence, it is worth remembering what critics of the day said: University of Chicago President Robert Maynard Hutchins archly predicted that if it were enacted it would turn American universities into "intellectual hobo jungles." How wrong he was and how evocative the quote sounds, particularly in the context of NCLB.

Finally, more important even than making the ethical—even moral—case on behalf of NCLB, Paul Kimmelman makes the pragmatic case for implementation, arguing as it were that practice is policy. Do NCLB correctly and schooling in America will be transformed. A welcome lesson for policy wonks like myself, it is nonetheless a difficult lesson for many mainline educators who have seen reforms come and go. Skeptical by temperament (and made more so by experience), many teachers have seen it all and characteristically respond with the admonition, this too shall pass. Kimmelman's strongest suit is that he speaks from hard-won experience in the trenches. He is one of their own, talking the talk because he has walked the walk.

* * * * *

This book makes a singularly important contribution to the debate about NCLB both by remarshalling the moral case and by forcefully and persuasively making the instrumental case. NCLB should be supported because it is the right and proper thing to do, Kimmelman reminds us. In a genuinely American and modern way, however, Kimmelman argues that NCLB is important for instrumental reasons as well. As a nation—from an economic and cultural perspective—we can afford to leave no one behind.

Indeed, to reconcile ourselves to leaving some behind is to set the stage for leaving everyone behind, the obverse, as it were, of the moving Hebrew admonition, he who saves one man saves the world entire.

As it is, we have the advantage of a comparative example—the Japanese economic miracle. It was fueled by an education miracle in which no Japanese were left behind. As Merry White, author of *The Japanese Educational Challenge* (1987), has noted, the Japanese have a secret trade weapon: their schools. They produce the best educated workforce in the world. For those who want empirical evidence, it is to be found in the following fact: Not content with having among the world's highest test scores, Japanese scores cluster around the mean. There are few outliers. Everyone does well in Japan. The implications of this are staggering, particularly in a world that is growing flat, as New York Times columnist Thomas Friedman reminds us. By this he means that we compete on a global basis, and the workers of a country who outperform the workers of another will enjoy their day in the sun. Their country will too.

In the final analysis, Kimmelman does something even more important than preaching the gospel of NCLB—he offers constructive suggestions and examples of how to not just deal with it but also make it work and make it work well. That, indeed, is the acid test to which NCLB will be put.

This is a must-read book for anyone who cares about NCLB. By owning up to the difficulty of implementation—and proffering real ideas for meeting NCLB's challenges—it provides the armature for essential reform and improvement efforts. Also, it reminds us of the power of the old political adage: Take care that the best does not become the enemy of the good.

Denis P. Doyle
Chevy Chase, Maryland

Preface

It has been approximately 4 years since Congress passed the most comprehensive federal education legislation since the first Elementary and Secondary Education Act (ESEA) it approved in 1965. Although not particularly significant, it is probably more of an irony that the first ESEA was signed into law by a Democratic president, Lyndon B. Johnson, and was intended to help disadvantaged children receive a higher quality education. The newest ESEA, the No Child Left Behind Act (NCLB), approved overwhelmingly by a bipartisan Congress, was signed into law by a Republican president, George W. Bush, in January 2002. NCLB was basically intended to require states to

1. have an accountability plan for benchmarked results using standards;

2. use proven programs that work;

3. ensure that teachers are qualified for their teaching assignments; and

4. narrow the achievement gap between disadvantaged children and their peers in U.S. schools.

Forty-nine years after the federal government became significantly involved in the operation of public schooling, it is still clear that education remains in the domain of both of America's major political parties. Despite the fact that the U.S. Constitution makes no mention of education, federal policymakers have gradually carved out a role for themselves that has transformed from merely offering funding to help disadvantaged students to proscribing a framework for accountability that demonstrates that all students are achieving proficiency on their states' assessments. Although not stipulating specifically what those assessments must measure, Congress was careful to apply a universal benchmark, the National Assessment of Education Progress, to determine the rigor of each state's education standards.

The No Child Left Behind Act has had an incredible response from educators and others interested in education. After more than 35 years as a teacher, assistant principal, principal, assistant superintendent, superintendent, consultant, and adjunct education professor, I cannot remember one instance when a federal education law had as much impact so quickly. Previous education laws and initiatives came and went; national commission reports were publicized and faded into relative oblivion. Consider the report, *A Nation at Risk* (U.S. Department of Education, 1983), warning of impending danger if U.S. schools did not improve. It seems like it received more attention in 2003, 20 years later, than it did when it was initially released. Also, it likely had more influence on education reform in 2003 than it did in 1983. Other reports, *Prisoners of Time* (National Education Commission on Time and Learning, 1994) and *Before It's Too Late—A Report to the Nation From the National Commission on Mathematics and Science Teaching for the 21st Century* (U.S. Department of Education, 2000) (a commission on which I served as a member), have had very limited influence on education reform. The National Commission on Mathematics and Science Teaching for the 21st Century was chaired by former astronaut and Ohio U.S. Senator John Glenn, an American icon from the days of America's first manned space program, Project Mercury. The commission also included the CEOs of Intel and State Farm Insurance; members of Congress; a governor; representatives from the National Aeronautics and Space Administration, the Defense Department, and the President's cabinet; as well as education practitioners. Despite the prestigious membership of the commission, it has had little impact on mathematics and science education reform.

Why is it that NCLB aroused so many people in both positive and negative ways? Was NCLB innovative or the result of many years of pent up frustration from business leaders and national and state policymakers regarding the low achievement of many U.S. students? Why did the education establishment protest many of the NCLB rules promulgated by the U.S. Department of Education? What strategies can be used to successfully implement NCLB to improve schools?

This book is an attempt to be a useful resource for understanding how NCLB became a law. More important, however, this book is intended to help educators realize that standards, accountability and assessment, teacher quality, parental options, and reforming schools were important but ignored issues for a long time before NCLB became a law. It is my hope that understanding what may well have been the mistakes of the past by not recognizing and implementing the trends or recommendations from policymakers and business leaders may prevent repeating the mistakes in the future. Certainly the recent and increased rhetoric from governors and business leaders on the need for high school reform is analogous to what I have attempted to offer in this book. Educators must understand the importance of building their organizational capacity and undertaking the process of reform on their own to prevent more policy mandates in the future. This book focuses on building organizational capacity through a knowledge model to meet the rigorous requirements of NCLB and to successfully implement school improvement initiatives (Figure A). It will not break new ground but, rather, will encourage practitioners to recognize the importance of acquiring, managing, and implementing knowledge to inform decision making. Instead of drawing on what might be perceived as a complex model, I have chosen to describe the concept in a simple, straightforward manner.

As you will realize, this book is different because it identifies organizational capacity as a three-part knowledge process. It is not a "cookbook" for education practitioners; instead, it is a contextual framework that should guide the process for developing professional wisdom. It is intended to be used by educators who have an

Figure A   Organizational Capacity-Building Knowledge Model

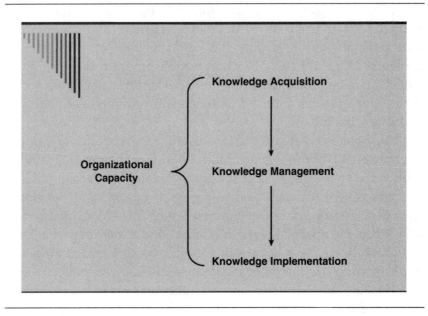

active role in leading their school or district improvement activities. The first step is a collaborative learning community that will focus on research and evidence-based practices. Board of education members, superintendents, principals, and teacher leaders will all find the information in this book useful as a starting point for their work. College professors can use it to encourage their students to create a mind-set for research- and evidence-based school reform initiatives.

It is important to set the context for change before organizations can respond to transformational work. John Kotter, a respected writer on change (Kotter & Cohen, 2002, p. 61), outlines important steps that must be taken before change can be implemented successfully. One of those steps is creating a vision. Clearly, NCLB lays out the vision Congress has for all students in the United States. To implement that vision, however, it is necessary to get "buy in" from the stakeholders. Unfortunately, that part of the process has not worked as well as policymakers had hoped. From the time NCLB became a law, it was not embraced by those who had to implement it. In Chapter 1, I provide an overview of the path that many of the education reforms traveled up to the time NCLB became a law. This will enable you to understand the context in which the law was passed.

In Chapters 2 through 5, I discuss the use of knowledge to build organizational capacity. To successfully improve schools will require an intense effort that is necessary to acquire, manage, and implement knowledge. Also, that knowledge must be credible and research and evidence based. I address the concept of building organizational capacity for successful implementation of NCLB and identify a variety of publications and products that can be used to build organizational capacity that can help practitioners with the daunting challenge of accountability for school improvement. This book is not intended to be a step-by-step guide to get you there but, instead, should be used as a starting point to set the context for continuous improvement to comply with the fundamental underpinnings of NCLB. I offer a plan with the hope that those charged with the task of school improvement will fill in the details.

Chapter 6 provides a mind-set for undertaking significant challenges. It was unrealistic for Congress and the U.S. Department of Education to think that, suddenly, every school and state in the country was going to rapidly embrace the notion that every student would make "adequate yearly progress" regardless of whether it was educationally possible, or that every school district would be able to ensure that all its teachers would be "highly qualified" by 2006. Although noble objectives, rather than accept the challenge, many educators and their organizations simply chose to put their energy into opposing the provisions of the law despite the fact that it was considered by many to be morally and ethically appropriate. I include stories about explorers and business leaders who confronted significant challenges and chose not to be defeated by them but instead to overcome them. These explorers and business leaders might be just like some of those unheralded teachers and school administrators who work in challenging situations but have remarkable success with their students. It is hoped that my examples will link your thinking in that context—examining how a positive mind-set makes a difference and how particular leadership styles affect overcoming insurmountable challenges.

Finally, successfully implementing NCLB is not about merely complying with rules and regulations but, rather, it is about building the capacity of teachers, administrators, and schools as organizations to continuously improve. Knowing how to be successful is the essential ingredient to achieve the challenging goals of NCLB. Even with the best curriculum, a teacher who lacks content knowledge and the necessary pedagogical skills will ultimately be ineffective.

A great deal can be learned from business leaders such as Jack Welch of General Electric, Lou Gerstner of IBM, and others who needed to transform their organizations during the 1990s to remain viable in a global economic society. Although they are from the business sector, their work can serve as a model for today's education leaders, who have similar daunting challenges to create a new standards-based, assessment-driven accountability culture in their districts and schools.

So where should we go from here? As noted previously, this book is not intended to be a cookbook for building the capacity to implement NCLB. Instead, it provides a knowledge model for building organizational capacity. It includes examples of current practices, research, suggestions, and reflective questions along with some theories and "envelope pushing" thoughts with the intent that they will be used by school learning and improvement teams to implement their own plans based on evidence- or research-based practices or both. Far too many school improvement initiatives begin by jumping on a new idea. Often, they are called the fad of the year. Also, school improvement leaders often implement them without setting a context for the project. For instance, they do not discuss why the project is necessary, how they can go about implementing it successfully in their own organizational culture, or research what others have done to succeed in similar circumstances.

I use examples for building organizational capacity from business and sports as well as education. The reason for this is because

I believe business, in particular, has undergone the cultural transformation that education is currently being challenged to go through. Sports teams offer excellent examples of how data and statistics are applied to analyzing performance. One need only consider how many successful businesses had to transform their business plans or face going out of business because of the Internet.

Many people are questioning the quality of the public education system. We only need to observe the growth in home schooling, charter schools, and private sector services to public school students using public funds and also the use of vouchers. There is also sufficient evidence, as noted in Chapter 1, that business leaders have been actively involved in setting the agenda for education with policymakers to ensure that the transformation will take place. Ideas and concepts such as continuous improvement based on benchmarks, worker quality improvement through professional development, and using resources wisely are all part of this transformation. Educators do not have to look long and far to know how difficult it is to raise funds both locally and at the state level to support programs. Difficult decisions are being made by education leaders regarding what programs to retain and what ones to eliminate. Business leaders have been doing this during the past decade, and educators can learn from their successes and failures.

This book offers a model that should guide school improvement work. The purpose of the knowledge model is to provide structure and focus to school improvement efforts. I believe that the menu for school improvement is far too eclectic to result in the type of organizational success that will lead to meeting the requirements of NCLB. Certainly, local politics and decision making play a significant role for the work in schools. There is also a critical need to specifically delineate what are the core essential priorities for educating students, however, and to focus on them with an intense improvement effort. There is more than enough anecdotal evidence pointing to the facts that effective teachers have the greatest influence on student learning, effective principals are essential for high achievement in their schools, and high-quality systemic leadership from superintendents that focuses on district performance and accountability is critically important for school success.

To successfully incorporate these three concepts in schools necessitates a plan that builds organizational capacity by using knowledge acquisition, knowledge management, and knowledge implementation. The movement to use more research and evidence in education decision making will require organizations to be smart, which will only be done through building organizational capacity by acquiring, managing, and using knowledge wisely.

Acknowledgments

There are many people who I wish to acknowledge for their assistance with this project. First, my wife, who pushed me to get this project done, did all of the first draft word processing and provided me her feedback on the content. I consider her a partner in my work.

I thank my colleagues at Learning Point Associates, who always engage me in meaningful conversations and are essential to my work as an adviser in the office of the CEO. They are an amazing group and give meaning to the concept of "cerebral" discussions on education topics. In particular, I thank Michele Fitzpatrick, who served as my internal editor and was always available to help me think my way through the obstacles; Tim Grover, who was instrumental in reviewing the final draft of the manuscript and diligently preparing the final copy; Claudette Rasmussen for her work on Resource A and Peggie Klekotka for her work on Resource B; and CEO Gina Burkhardt, who always pushes me to reach higher goals and has modeled for us what it takes to transform an organization.

I extend a special thank-you to Denis Doyle for writing the Foreword and providing feedback to me on the content of the book. Andy Rotherham and Ken Arndt offered their thoughts as I was writing and are trusted colleagues and friends; I have watched both of them achieve amazing success in their careers. My periodontist brother, Dr. James Kimmelman, also took an unusual interest in this book and read every page to give me his opinions. Knowing him, it was just the right opportunity to spend his spare time criticizing me. I also thank my daughter Leah, an elementary school principal, for her advice and help on this book. Also, I would be remiss if I did not say how proud I am of my daughter Renee, who works in the corporate offices of Esteé Lauder, and my son-in-law Scott, who is at the corporate offices of American Express.

Thanks to Dan Ginsberg from SchoolNet and Pamela Kislak from the Northwest Evaluation Association for their assistance in helping me accurately describe their products, which are good examples of knowledge management. Also to Rebecca Herman from the American Institutes for Research for her assistance with the section on the What Works Clearinghouse.

While I am recognizing special people, I mention Congressman Mark Kirk and Congresswoman Judy Biggert and their dedicated staffs. Mr. Kirk and Ms. Biggert have made my vision for an NCLB implementation center that is focused on helping schools improve a reality. Without them, it would not have been possible. In addition, I owe a debt of gratitude to all the members of Congress and their staffs who give me their valuable time and advice on education issues. They deserve far more credit than they receive.

Finally, I thank Rachel Livsey, my Corwin editor, who I actually believe intimidated me into completing this project. I cannot say I enjoy writing books, but I made a commitment to her—so here is my thinking on education reform.

The contributions of the following reviewers are gratefully acknowledged:

Michael Fullan
Professor of Policy Studies
University of Toronto
Toronto, Ontario, Canada

Roberta E. Glaser
Teacher
St. Johns Public Schools
St. Johns, MI

Elizabeth J. Lolli
Superintendent
Barberton City School District
Barberton, OH

Carole Cooper
Coordinator for Student
   Achievement
Community School District 300
Carpentersville, IL

Theron J. Schutte
Superintendent
Boone Community
   School District
Boone, IA

About the Author

Paul L. Kimmelman is Senior Adviser to the CEO at Learning Point Associates. He has served as a consultant to the Qualifications and Curriculum Authority in England and senior consultant to Project 2061 Professional Development Programs of the American Association for the Advancement of Science. He worked in K–12 education for more than 30 years as a teacher, assistant high school principal, middle school principal, assistant superintendent, and superintendent, and he has been an adjunct professor at several colleges and universities. Currently, he is Adjunct Professor at Argosy University. As superintendent in Lima, Ohio, he worked to help the district successfully comply with a federal desegregation order. He served as president of the First in the World Consortium when he was a superintendent in Illinois. The consortium was a collaborative group of school districts that were the first noncountry group to participate in the Third International Mathematics and Science Study. He has authored numerous articles and publications on education and presented at national and state education meetings. He is coauthor (with D. Kroeze) of *Achieving World-Class Schools: Mastering School Improvement Using a Genetic Model* (2002). He was appointed by former U.S. Secretary of Education Richard Riley to the National Commission on Mathematics and Science Teaching, chaired by former senator and astronaut John Glenn, and served on the Third International Mathematics and Science Study Technical Review Panel. He was also appointed by U.S. Secretary of Education Rod Paige to serve on the Teacher Assistance Corps and participated in the Teacher-to-Teacher project offering sessions on building teacher leaders. He also serves as an advisory board member for the National Council on Teacher Quality.

1

Education Events
That Led to NCLB

The requirements of the No Child Left Behind Act (NCLB) seemed to come as a surprise to many educators. More astonishing was the fact that many of them paid little attention to the law after it was passed in January 2002. It was not until some of the sanctions became known and their schools were confronted with potential loss of funds or identified as needing improvement that parents began to take notice. It was not until schools were being required to allow students to transfer to other schools or to allow students to receive supplemental services from commercial providers, or even potentially being required to change curricula or staff and have teachers demonstrate subject knowledge competency, that a "rebellion" began. The National Education Association, a major teachers' union, and the American Association of School Administrators, an organization that represents school superintendents and other professional organizations, began an ongoing public relations onslaught against what they believed were problems with some provisions of the law. To be fair, they did not condemn the fundamental principles contained within NCLB but, rather, complained about the accountability and sanction provisions. Schools that for many years had a large majority of their students meeting proficiency on their state assessments and that were recognized as excellent schools were being identified as "in need of improvement" because they failed to make adequate yearly progress (AYP). NCLB required all schools to disaggregate student achievement data, and those students who did not do well in the "other" schools did not tend to do well in the so-called "better schools" either. Also, teachers who had taught for many years were being required to demonstrate subject matter competency in the core academic subjects they taught. These concepts were foreign to the U.S. school culture and thus met with serious opposition from some state education agencies, professional education organizations, and educators in general. To be certain, some of the arguments that were being raised were logical and could inform the future reauthorization of NCLB, or at least have some influence on how the U.S. Department of Education implements the law, but complaints about various provisions of the law were distracting from its fundamental principles—to improve student achievement and raise the requirements for teacher qualifications in the United States.

Although some of the concerns were justified, it is unfortunate that the energy devoted to addressing the problems with the law far exceeded the energy needed to confront the challenges of educating all students. Changing organizational culture in schools is not an easy task. Yet, the performance of U.S. students is not very good compared to that of their international student counterparts on a variety of assessments. The most frequently cited assessment to support the contention that U.S. students did poorly compared to other international students is the Third International Mathematics and Science Study (TIMSS) (www.TIMSS.org). This assessment found that although U.S. 4th-grade students tended to do fairly well in mathematics and science, 8th- and 12th-grade students did poorly compared to students in other countries. Also, the longer U.S. students remained in school, the worse they performed in mathematics and science compared to their international counterparts.

Another international assessment in which U.S. students have had disappointing achievement is the Program for Student Assessment (PISA) (www.pisa.oecd.org). This assessment measures 15-year-old students' knowledge and skills that are essential for full participation in society in reading, mathematical, and scientific literacy. One important difference between PISA and TIMSS is that PISA is also intended to measure if the students have the knowledge and skills needed in adult life. Thus, federal policymakers set new standards through NCLB that were going to be enforced by the U.S. Secretary of Education. Those new standards would require a new culture in schools of using data and research to improve the academic achievement of students and change the requirements for teacher qualifications.

One of the key issues with NCLB was the implementation process. Those educators charged with the task of NCLB compliance need to know that when leading the change process, it is important to set a context and gain support for the changes. Although there was substantial opposition to NCLB from educators, and in some instances for good reasons, the fact is that since the Soviet Union launched the first space satellite, Sputnik, in 1957, there have been a number of education activities and reports that ultimately became the core requirements of it. It is difficult to believe that for almost 50 years the federal government was gradually assuming a greater role in public education and that so many federal and state policymakers, governors in particular, business leaders, and education commissions were calling for massive changes and nothing of significance was actually happening.

First, students from poverty, certain racial groups, students with limited English proficiency, and students with disabilities continued to fall increasingly further behind their higher achieving peers. Second, teachers continued to be assigned to classroom teaching responsibilities they were unprepared to teach. Also, the costs for education continued to increase as well as funding from governmental sources to pay for it. Unfortunately, student achievement results did not improve enough with the increased funding. Thus, NCLB became law, with considerable debate and publicity following.

What were the initiatives and reports that should have been a warning that substantial policy changes were forthcoming? Why wasn't there a clear explanation of how those initiatives and reports led to NCLB? Most of the arguments being raised against NCLB were not about its fundamental principles but, rather, the accountability provisions. The attitude of many educators was simply that they did not believe the law's expectations were realistic.

Thus, considerable time was devoted to the debate over ideology instead of addressing the key issues and what realistically could be done to narrow or even close the achievement gap in the United States. It is one thing to say that all students should be able to achieve proficiency on state assessments and yet quite another to believe that those who have severe cognitive disabilities or are unable to speak English will achieve the same results as their more able peers. That debate needs to be clarified. Clearly, the foundation for the 100% achievement requirement for all students was not carefully planned with those who were expected to implement it.

The following events and reports are not intended to be all-inclusive but, rather, to provide a brief description and evidence that for more than four decades, policymakers, business leaders, and leading education reformers were putting "blips on the education radar screen" that were basically going undetected by the education profession. The failure to respond to them ultimately led to a law that many educators do not understand, do not agree with, or do not know how to go about implementing. In addition, the process used by the U.S. Department of Education promulgating rules and regulations and disseminating basic information about NCLB was slow and often unclear. State and local school district officials were not getting the information they needed, but more effort could have been made by them to understand the basic provisions of the law. It is my belief that having some background on the history of these activities and reports will help resolve some of the complaints about it and enable educators to avoid making the same mistakes of complacency in the future.

NCLB will most likely be considered for reauthorization in 2007. Most federal laws of the magnitude of NCLB need revision over time to fit the diverse fabric of the country and their intended outcomes. If one is looking for examples, certainly Medicare and Social Security continue to be debated and are still the subject of philosophical differences among policymakers and recipients. Ironically, it is some of the concerns with NCLB that are being discussed among educators that will likely be some of the revisions when the law is reauthorized. More important, the revisions will be based on evidence, an important concept in the law.

Activities and Reports

Sputnik—1957

Until 1957, education in the United States was the sole responsibility of the states. In fact, there is no mention of education in the U.S. Constitution. Yet when the Soviet Union launched the first space satellite, Sputnik, on October 4, 1957, President Dwight Eisenhower called for training more scientists and engineers. In 1958, the U.S. Congress passed the National Defense Education Act (NDEA). Using national security as the basis for the law, Congress determined that the problem with the United States falling behind the Soviet Union was the result of the education system, particularly mathematics and science education.

Interestingly, there are some parallel issues with the enactment of NDEA and NCLB. First, in both instances there was concern about the federal government becoming involved in public education. This issue was overcome because new funds were an attractive incentive to schools to accept reforms. Second, the primary theme was the space race and rocketry, but teachers had little knowledge about space or teaching resources to integrate them into the curriculum. Sound familiar? Now, approximately 50 years later, the federal government is becoming more involved in public education through NCLB and is using funding as an incentive to force schools to improve or face sanctions—and the emphasis is still on mathematics and science education. There is a real need to offer more support to school administrators and teachers so they understand NCLB and gain the skills in the use of data, standards-based instruction, and evidence-based pedagogy to ensure student learning success.

Life Magazine—1958

In 1958, there was not the plethora of magazine choices for consumers as there are today. The staple of the day was *Life* magazine. With its wide distribution, *Life* did a three-part series on the "crisis in American education." Overall, the series concluded that teachers were "wretchedly overworked, underpaid, and disregarded" ("Crisis in American Education," 1958). Two other key points in the series should resonate with what NCLB requires: The articles stated that teachers did not have enough time to plan lessons and a "discouraging number of them are incompetent."

Those two points became part of NCLB's teacher quality provisions. First, there are funds in Title II to provide research-based professional development to improve the quality of teachers and principals. Second, teachers are expected to meet highly qualified provisions set by each state that include at least a bachelor's degree, full state certification, and demonstrated subject knowledge competency in the courses they teach. It seems ironic that these same issues that were important in 1958 are still being discussed in the same context today, half a century later.

Elementary and Secondary Education Act of 1965

If the National Defense Education Act of 1958 laid the cornerstone for federal involvement in public education, then the Elementary and Secondary Education Act of 1965 (ESEA) "built the house." ESEA was part of President Lyndon B. Johnson's Great Society program. The basic purpose of ESEA was to provide assistance to children from low-income families. Throughout the years, federal funding for schools has continued to increase, and these funds are serving more than just children from low-income families. Despite the increases in federal funding for the programs, students from low-income families continue to do poorly in school. Interestingly, during the past 40 years, students from low-income families have fallen further behind their more affluent suburban peers. It is this "achievement gap" that ultimately led to the concept of NCLB and disaggregating data by subgroup. The idea that no child could be left behind is monitored by requiring achievement data on the performance of the student subgroups.

A Nation at Risk—1983

In 1983, Secretary of Education Terrell Bell released *A Nation at Risk: The Imperative for Educational Reform* (U.S. Department of Education, 1983). This report was based on the findings from the National Commission on Excellence in Education, a commission Bell created to help define the problems with U.S. education and to recommend solutions. A quote in the report summarizes the seriousness of the problem according to the commission: "Our society is being eroded by a rising tide of mediocrity that threatens our very future as a nation and a people" (p. 5).

Again, similar to what happened in 1958 with NDEA, education was being cited as the reason for the United States being confronted with serious problems. If education was not improved, there would be consequences in the future. The commission that issued this report was composed of prestigious and influential members, including representatives from business, higher education, state education agencies, and K–12 practitioners. Although it had the "bully pulpit" of the secretary of education, there still was not much education reform.

One other quote from the report should also be considered significant. The commission noted that "(i)f an unfriendly foreign power had attempted to impose on America the mediocre educational performance that exists today, we might well have viewed it as an act of war" (U.S. Department of Education, 1983, p. 5).

The report included a number of indicators of the risks if there was no support for the commission's recommendations, including unfavorable comparisons of U.S. student achievement with their international peers, the large number of adults and 17-year-olds who were functionally illiterate, the declining achievement of high school students on standardized achievement tests, and the concerns of business and military leaders with regard to the costs for remedial education for the students they were hiring. The report called for the following:

- Increased high school graduation requirements
- Schools, colleges, and universities to adopt more rigorous and measurable standards, and higher expectations for academic performance and student conduct
- Significantly more time be devoted to the learning of the new basics, including consideration of a longer school day and year
- Improve the preparation of teachers and make teaching more rewarding and respected
- Citizens to hold their elected officials and educators responsible for providing the leadership necessary to achieve the recommendations

Many of the ideas and concepts contained in *A Nation at Risk* are included in NCLB. For example, NCLB requires high schools to maintain data on their graduation rates; states must write academic standards and administer assessments to measure whether students are meeting them; there are sanctions for schools that fail to meet certain progress requirements for students, including provisions stipulating that teachers and principals can be removed from the schools that do not meet them; and implementing improved professional development for principals and teachers based on practices that have evidence of success.

Although there is scant evidence that the depth of the reforms called for in *A Nation at Risk* actually took place, it is clear that policymakers incorporated some of the recommendations from it in NCLB. The fact that Congress and the President called for rigid enforcement of NCLB was also an indication that the quotes from *A Nation at Risk* regarding the mediocrity of U.S. education were being taken seriously by them.

1989 President's Education Summit

Prior to 1989, there was an effort by President Ronald Reagan to abolish the Department of Education; that effort failed. When George H. W. Bush became president, he convened governors, some members of his cabinet, and a few high-level administration officials for an education summit. Although the process was bipartisan, it was not always amicable (Achieve, 1999). Interestingly, one of the leaders of the summit was former Arkansas governor and future president William J. Clinton.

The 1989 summit, citing the *Nation at Risk* report, took it to another level by promoting national education goals. Of significance is the fact that the federal role in education was continuing to increase, with greater involvement in state and local policies and even suggesting national education goals. At the summit, President George H. W. Bush and the nation's governors agreed to the following:

- Establish a process for setting national education goals
- Seek greater flexibility and enhanced accountability in the use of federal resources to meet the goals, through both regulatory and legislative changes
- Undertake a major state-by-state effort to restructure the education system
- Report annually on progress in achieving the goals

The participants went on to agree that a task force overseen by the National Governors' Association would work with the President's designees to recommend goals by 1990. The framework for the goals would, if achieved, guarantee that the United States would be internationally competitive related to

- readiness of children to start school;
- the performance of students on international achievement tests, especially in math and science;
- the reduction of the dropout rate and the improvement of academic performance, especially among at-risk students;
- the functional literacy of adult Americans;

- the level of training necessary to guarantee a competitive workforce;
- the supply of qualified teachers and up-to-date technology; and
- the establishment of safe, disciplined, and drug-free schools.

Furthermore, the summit concluded that states must focus on the achievement of all students, raise academic standards, and be responsible for improving them: "The time for rhetoric is past; the time for performance is now" (Achieve, 1999). Many of those recommendations are included in NCLB. They include dropout rate reduction, safe schools, qualified teachers, performance assessment, and higher standards. Despite the fact that the President convened this summit and many governors from both parties participated, the results were similar to those obtained in the past— that is, very little was done by educators to address their concerns. The simple fact was that the education profession was consistently being advised of potentially serious problems by people who could enact new education policy. Unfortunately, little was done to address their concerns.

National Commission on Time and Learning—1994

The National Commission on Time and Learning was created by a federal law, the Education Council Act of 1991. The Act called for an independent advisory body to conduct a comprehensive review of the relationship between time and learning in the nation's schools. A nine-member panel—three appointed by the secretary of education, three by the president of the Senate, and three by speaker of the House of Representatives—was charged with the responsibility to submit a report by April 1994. Not surprisingly, the panel concluded that

(t)ime is the missing element in our great national debate about learning and the need for higher standards for all students. Our schools and the people involved with them—students, teachers, administrators, parents, and staff—are prisoners of time, captives of the school clock and calendar.

The report explained that for 150 years, U.S. public schools held time constant and let learning vary. Interestingly, the commission used a quote similar to the one used in *A Nation at Risk*. It quoted Oliver Hazard Perry, who said in a dispatch from the War of 1812, "We have met the enemy and they are (h)ours (sic)."

The Perry quote used by the commission, along with the quote from *A Nation at Risk* stating that our society was being eroded by a rising tide of mediocrity, demonstrates the seriousness others were placing on the unacceptable performance of U.S. education. It was apparent, however, that seriousness was not shared by many in the education community. The achievement performance of U.S. students continued to decline, and major accountability reform activities were not being undertaken. The Commission on Time and Learning made eight recommendations:

- Reinvent schools around learning, not time.
- Fix the design flaw: Use time in new and better ways.
- Establish an academic day.
- Keep schools open longer to meet the needs of children and communities.
- Give teachers the time they need.
- Invest in technology.
- Develop local action plans to transform schools.
- Share the responsibility; finger pointing and evasion must end.

These recommendations, along with the other reports, were setting a context for much needed reform to traditional education practices. Whereas NCLB does not proscribe how schools must reach the goals, the study on time clearly described how difficult it would be to achieve the required success without considering structural changes to the school day and year.

The commission's report was followed by a study released by the U.S. Department of Education in 1996 titled *The Uses of Time for Teaching and Learning* (Adelman, 1996). This study was organized to examine three aspects of educational time:

- The quantity of time in school
- The quality of time in school
- Student's use of out-of-school time

The study explored the issues raised by the commission, but for the most part the inefficient use of time in schools continues to be a critical issue for school leaders and teachers.

In October 2005, the Education Commission of the States released an update on the recommendations from the 1994 commission report (Goldberg & Cross, 2005). The report stated that "little has changed regarding time for formal schooling" since the first report was issued more than a decade ago (p. 2). The length of the school day and that of the school year remain virtually the same in most schools today as they did throughout the 20th century.

One new aspect of the report is the emphasis on technology. It is emphasized that students now live in a digital world and use the Internet, cell phones, and digital devices to access information and accelerate communications. The report calls for not only more learning time but also new and better ways of using it.

The release of a new report more than 10 years after the original report acknowledging that not much happens supports the premise I have used as an overarching theme for this chapter: Many call for education reform, but not much happens.

Goals 2000—1994

There is some irony in the fact that President George H. W. Bush, a Republican, convened the 1989 President's Education Summit and it was cochaired by Arkansas Governor William J. Clinton, a Democrat who then defeated Bush in the 1993 presidential election. One cornerstone of the Clinton administration agenda was education, emboldened by the reauthorization of the ESEA and known as Goals 2000, a law containing a number of principles from the summit convened by President Bush. President Clinton appointed the former governor of South Carolina, Richard Riley, to be his secretary of education, and the plan from President Bush's summit was to become the basis for Clinton's education agenda. Goals 2000 set national goals that called for

- school readiness;
- school completion;
- student academic achievement;
- leadership in mathematics and science;
- adult literacy; and
- safe and drug-free schools.

Although most of the goals were topics that historically addressed education issues regarding student achievement, the list added safe and drug-free schools. This issue was rather new and only added to the tasks with which schools were already struggling.

Clearly, Goals 2000 was the actual forerunner to NCLB. The cornerstone of the NCLB reauthorization was contained in Goals 2000. Congress and President Clinton had truly set the stage for more federal involvement in state and local education policy.

1996 National Education Summit

Governors from more than 40 states and national business leaders met on March 26 and 27, 1996, to discuss the state of U.S. education. It was the sense of many of the nation's business leaders that the U.S. education system was in need of significant change, and since the educators had not taken it upon themselves to do it, the task would fall upon others who could. The summit was led by Louis Gerstner, then chairman and CEO of IBM. Of note is the fact that no education organizations were invited to participate in this summit. The summit briefing materials provided background on seven key questions:

- Why do we need high academic standards?
- Does the public support high academic standards and accountability?
- Does the business community support high academic standards and accountability?
- Do other nations have academic standards and is the United States competitive?
- What exactly is a standard?
- How much progress has been made by the states in their efforts to implement high academic standards, assessment, and accountability?
- How can technology be an effective tool to help students and schools reach high academic standards?

These seven questions clearly delineated the trends in education that had been emerging and the emphasis that business leaders and governors were going to place on them to ensure that changes took place in state education systems. It was apparent that standards, assessment, and accountability, key provisions of NCLB, and international comparisons of student achievement would be used to determine how well U.S. students were doing in core subjects. In addition, how technology could effectively be implemented to improve the process of education was going to continue to receive attention from these individuals, who believed they could actually make changes in a system that had been resisting them for many years.

The governors and business leaders left their summit recommending that there be clear academic standards and better subject matter content at the state and local levels. No longer were they viewing U.S. education as separate and distinct by states; they were now working within a national paradigm.

National Commission on Teaching and America's Future—1996

The National Commission on Teaching and America's Future (1996) operated on the basis of three premises:

- What teachers know and can do is the most important influence on what students learn.
- Recruiting, preparing, and retaining good teachers is the central strategy to improving our schools.
- School reform cannot succeed unless it focuses on creating the conditions under which teachers can teach and teach well.

The commission set a goal for implementation of its recommendations by 2006. What was particularly eye opening was what the commission saw as the barriers to achieving its recommendations. It noted that there were low expectations for student performance, unenforced standards for teachers, major flaws in teacher preparation, painfully slipshod teacher recruitment, inadequate induction for beginning teachers, lack of professional development and rewards for knowledge and skill, and schools that were structured for failure rather than success. Again, the themes were eerily similar, with nothing new being added to the proposals for school reform:

- Get serious about standards for both students and teachers.
- Reinvent teacher preparation and professional development.
- Fix teacher recruitment, and put qualified teachers in every classroom.
- Encourage and reward teacher knowledge and skill.
- Create schools that are organized for student and teacher success.

Noteworthy from this commission was its complete and total focus on teaching. All its recommendations and the acknowledged barriers reinforced what had been said about the problems with U.S. education for many years.

1999 National Education Summit

The 1999 National Education Summit included approximately 30 governors, business executives, and educators. Three core principles were the focus of the summit:

1. Reform begins with a commitment to set the highest academic standards.

2. Quality assessments are essential to measure progress against those standards.

3. Implementation of comprehensive systems is required to guarantee full accountability for results, starting with real improvements in student achievement (Achieve, 1999).

The participants at this summit affirmed their commitment to raising student achievement to world-class standards. They also set a 6-month deadline for states to respond to the summit action statement urging progress on the following key challenges:

- Improve educator quality
- Help all students achieve high standards
- Strengthen accountability

It is apparent that the gradual and consistent evolution of the call for rigorous standards, accountability, and improving teacher quality was gaining a foothold with an increasing number of people. To improve educator quality, the participants committed to

- strengthen entrance and exit requirements of teacher education programs;
- target professional development programs that give teachers the content knowledge and skills to teach to higher standards; and
- develop competitive salary structures to attract and retain the best qualified teachers and school leaders with pay for skills and performance.

To help all students achieve high standards, the participants agreed to work together in states to ensure that every school had a rigorous curriculum and professional development program aligned with state standards and tests, expand public school choice and charter schools, and develop extended day and year programs for students at risk.

To strengthen accountability, they agreed to work together in the states to create incentives for success and consequences for failure, strengthen the ability of principals and teachers to select their own colleagues and control school budgets, provide students who were at risk of failure with opportunities for extra help, and recognize highly successful schools and intervene in low-performing schools.

These commitments were all a significant part of NCLB. It would be logical to conclude that the work of the 1999 National Education Summit had a significant influence on the law. For educators, the recommendations from the summit should have served as notice that policymakers were getting more serious about what they believed were the needed reforms with respect to the weaknesses in U.S. education and that more should have been undertaken by educators to address them.

National Commission on Mathematics and Science Teaching for the 21st Century—2000

In 1999, Secretary of Education Richard Riley appointed a commission to make recommendations for improving mathematics and science teaching in the 21st century. Since Sputnik, there had been a steady stream of reports calling for improvements in U.S. student achievement in both of these subjects. The National Commission on Mathematics and Science Teaching, known as the Glenn Commission (named for its chairman, former astronaut and Ohio senator John Glenn), began its work with the knowledge that U.S student achievement in mathematics and science was far from acceptable after reviewing students' performance on the (TIMSS). TIMSS provided data that demonstrated that the longer U.S. students remained in school, their performance declined in mathematics and science compared with students from other countries. Although U.S. students did fairly well in both subjects in 4th grade, their performance declined considerably by the time they reached 8th and 12th grades.

The Glenn Commission identified four key points and made three recommendations (U.S. Department of Education, 2000). First, the commission was convinced that the future well-being of the nation and people depends not just on how well we educate our children generally but also, specifically, on how well we educate them in mathematics and science. Again, the future of the nation was superimposed in a major education report citing the importance of education in solving a critical national problem.

Second, it is abundantly clear from the evidence that we are not doing the job that we should do—or can do—in teaching our children to understand and use ideas from these fields. After Sputnik, a number of education reports emphasized that the quality of mathematics and science education was not of an acceptable caliber for U.S. students to be globally competitive. The Glenn Commission actually reemphasized much of what *Life* magazine wrote in 1958.

Third, after an extensive, in-depth review of what was happening in U.S. classrooms, the commission concluded that the most powerful instrument for change, and therefore the place to begin, was at the very core of education—with teaching. Very few reports prior to this included the importance of teaching in their recommendations. During the previous 40 years, there was minimal change in teacher preparation programs and ongoing learning opportunities in professional development for teachers, despite the increasing complexity of actually teaching mathematics and science.

Fourth, the commission believed that committing the nation to reach three specific goals could go far in bringing about the needed basic changes. The goals went directly to the issues of quality, quantity, and an enabling work environment for teachers of mathematics and science. The commission issued three recommendations:

1. Establish an ongoing system to improve the quality of mathematics and science teaching in grades K–12.

2. Increase significantly the number of mathematics and science teachers, and improve the quality of their preparation.

3. Improve the working environment, and make the teaching profession more attractive for K–12 mathematics and science teachers.

2001 National Education Summit

The 2001 National Education Summit was held in October despite being scheduled so soon after the catastrophic events of the September 11 terrorist attacks. The fact that the summit was held affirms the serious commitment the participants had for reforming U.S. education. The opening page of the briefing book explained their position regarding the meeting (Achieve, 2001):

> The governors, corporate leaders, and educators who organized this meeting extend their deepest sympathies to those who lost loved ones in the terrorist assaults of September 11th. Events of that day have profoundly affected every American. The people of the United States can draw on great reservoirs of patriotism, decency, courage, and resilience as they respond to this unpardonable tragedy. The participants in this meeting, united in the belief that healthy public schools are the foundation of our democracy, dedicate this Summit to the task of building a stronger America.

Like the other compelling statements about the security of the United States in 1957 after the launch of Sputnik, about society being eroded in 1983 in *A Nation at Risk,* and the Oliver Hazard Perry quote used in the National Commission on Time and Learning report in 1994, the 2001 National Education Summit began with an affirmation that U.S. education was an important part of creating national success in a global environment and its decline was a serious problem for the country. This summit was the third time in 5 years that prestigious policymakers and corporate executives gathered to discuss education. Certainly, the fact that they were devoting so much time and attention to education was a clear signal that significant policy changes to reform public education were on the way. Also, not long after this summit convened in October, President George W. Bush and a bipartisan leadership group from Congress met to finalize NCLB.

The rationale for the 2001 summit was to support the goal of high standards. The participants' briefing book acknowledged that although there were examples of schools turning things around, the goal of high standards for all had not been met (Achieve, 2001). They also acknowledged that the President and Congress were poised to enact legislation that would accelerate the pace of the reforms they were recommending. Interestingly, they noted that states were "working hard but they would have to work even harder in the months and years ahead" (p. iii).

The three primary categories for this summit were public support, teaching, and learning as it related to closing the achievement gap and using data to drive improvement from testing and accountability. With respect to the belief that there was public opposition to standards and testing, the participants at the summit were told that the claims were overblown. Their report noted that testing represented a "minor investment of time for a worthwhile goal." They affirmed their belief that schools needed to use standards to raise achievement and not narrow instruction. Their support for standards was based on the notion that higher standards would raise expectations for student learning. Furthermore, they believed testing would be the best way to measure progress toward attaining the standards.

To close the achievement gap, the commission cited a number of characteristics of successful schools. It noted that researchers identified the following characteristics from those schools:

- A relentless focus on academic performance for all students
- A shared sense among the faculty and staff that they are all responsible for the learning of every student
- Frequent and regular assessment of student progress for diagnostic purposes
- Principals who are true instructional leaders
- A flexible use of time

As primarily policymakers, members of the commission discussed how states could improve instruction by creating a supportive policy environment. Their recommendations were clearly aligned with the provisions that would be contained in NCLB. First, they called for clear standards: "The best standards are clear, are measurable, and provide appropriate guidance to teachers, parents, and test developers. They are comprehensive yet allow for in-depth treatment of essential content" (Achieve, 2001, p. 16).

Another familiar discussion in the commission report was the use of disaggregated assessment data, ultimately a provision in NCLB that has become quite controversial. The report said that "(d)isaggregated testing data by race/ethnicity, income, special education status, and limited English proficiency is essential" (Achieve, 2001, p. 16). The commission noted that simply knowing that a certain percentage of students in a school meet standards can hide differences among students that may never be remedied.

Finally, the commission emphasized the importance of attracting and retaining qualified educators. It discussed the fact that too often the students who needed the best teachers were taught by those teachers who had the least experience and qualifications. To close the achievement gap, that problem had to be rectified (Achieve, 2001, p. 17).

Professional development also received considerable attention. Commission members recognized that the movement to a standards-based, assessment-driven education reform would require professional learning opportunities for teachers. Interestingly, they noted that in other professions (i.e., law and medicine), such opportunities are provided routinely. In addition, they mentioned that onetime workshops were not the answer, and that educational professional development was often ineffective because it was delivered in ineffective ways (Achieve, 2001, p. 18).

The 2001 National Education Summit recommendations came the closest to modeling what would become NCLB. The last of these summits brought together the concepts that became the fundamental underpinnings of NCLB.

No Child Left Behind Act—2001

In January 2002, President George W. Bush signed into law NCLB, the most comprehensive federal education law ever written and one that imposed serious sanctions for states and schools that failed to abide by its provisions. It was clear that our nation's leading policymakers, both Democrats and Republicans, were serious about ensuring that schools would improve the achievement of their students.

This book is not intended to be an overview of NCLB but instead offers a model for building the organizational capacity to comply with its provisions. Arguably, the real goal is for schools to improve and base their improvement work on practices and programs that have evidence they work. Nonetheless, it is important to summarize the basic ideas contained in NCLB to set the context for the remainder of this book.

NCLB is intended to improve the achievement of U.S. students by requiring states to write rigorous standards and assessments to measure whether students are meeting those standards. The assessments are required to provide data that are disaggregated by subgroups so that educators can make informed decisions regarding the appropriate actions to take to ensure that all students successfully meet their state's proficiency standards. Even schools with one subgroup not meeting those proficiency standards can be identified as "in need of improvement." The law emphasizes accountability, a concept that was consistently identified during approximately the past 50 years in most education reports as essential for improving schools so that all students meet proficiency standards.

Flexibility and local control are part of NCLB, despite complaints from many state and local educators that it actually takes away their decision-making authority. In defense of the states, it would be beneficial if they had timely knowledge of what other states submitted to the U.S. Department of Education and received approval for rather than keeping them in the dark on what is acceptable in their compliance plans. There is no formal, expedient process to find out what other states received approval for to help inform them of what might be acceptable in their plans. There is clearly a need for continuity with respect to the acceptable standards that states are required to meet in their compliance plans. Finally, the law allows some states and schools the flexibility to transfer their federal funds to other purposes if approved by the U.S. Department of Education.

The idea of focusing on what works is embedded in NCLB. Using scientifically based research is mentioned more than 100 times in the law. Congress was serious about the use of research- or evidenced-based programs in schools and reauthorized the former Office of Education Research and Improvement into the Institute of Education Sciences (IES) when it approved the Education Sciences Reform Act of 2002 after NCLB. The IES is developing a What Works Clearinghouse on its Web site (www.w-w-c.org) to help educators identify programs that have met research-based criteria to help them make decisions on what interventions to adopt in their schools.

Finally, NCLB requires states to set standards for determining highly qualified teachers. Many of the reports issued throughout the years indicated that the students who needed the most qualified teachers were being taught by teachers with less experience and often not fully certified for their teaching assignment. NCLB requires teachers in core subjects to have a bachelor's degree, full state certification, and to demonstrate subject matter competency. The states are allowed considerable latitude in determining the process to meet these requirements through their High Objective Uniform State Standards of Evaluation (HOUSSE).

In sum, NCLB incorporates the concepts that were discussed for many years and imposes sanctions for failing to meet certain requirements. Clearly, the law incorporates accountability, assessment, academic standards, and teacher quality as its cornerstones. All four of these concepts have been subjects of concern in nearly every report on education since 1957.

Summary

The No Child Left Behind Act became law in 2002 and thus began the implementation of education reform concepts that had been discussed in many meetings and reports since 1957. What was new this time, however, was that NCLB included serious sanctions for those states and schools that did not take "educating all students to meet their standards with qualified teachers" seriously. For nearly 50 years, the numerous commissions, studies, and reports have been remarkably similar in their recommendations and consistent in their call for improving U.S. education. It was not until the governors and business executives started their series of three national summits, however, that the policymaking process began to address requiring the changes being proposed. In many respects, NCLB is the culmination of all the reports and commissions' work. The themes are remarkably similar—accountability for all students learning, rigorous academic standards, assessment aligned to those standards, high-quality professional development, improved teacher preparation, and highly qualified teachers.

Knowing that most of these ideas have deep historical roots in the calls for education reform, there is no excuse that not much education reform was implemented that resulted in significant improvement in U.S. education during the past four decades. Now that many of those reforms are written into the NCLB law, what can be done to build organizational capacity to produce successful results? As a metaphor, U.S. education is not unlike the U.S. auto industry. The auto industry suffered from poor quality and an inability to compete with foreign competitors not too many years ago. It took time for the industry to transform itself and make the needed changes to improve its quality to even compete with foreign carmakers. For U.S. education to improve, the concepts of schooling will need to undergo significant change based on contemporary organizational thinking and building the capacity of workers to implement those changes. These thoughts are not intended to be perceived as a "bashing" of U.S. education but, rather, as a call to action to successfully meet the challenges imposed by NCLB.

An Action Idea

Spend time with your school improvement team discussing the key reform ideas, not only from the past but also what is being proposed in the future. This chapter described in detail some of the reforms pertaining to education standards, assessment and accountability, teacher quality, and closing the achievement gap. On the horizon is the call to reform high schools. President George H. W. Bush proposed a legislative initiative for high school reform in 2005, but it did not receive much attention from Congress. Business leaders and governors, however, are taking an active role in promoting the reform. Although the concept of reforming high schools may be a popular theme, what that reform means must be clearly defined. For example, is the reform for smaller schools, for more rigorous curriculums, or for new programs to prepare students for the workforce? In a poll conducted by the Alliance for Excellent Education, 83% of respondents believed improving high schools was extremely urgent or very urgent compared to only 79% for middle schools and 76% for elementary schools (Shek, 2005).

One action step to do now: Facilitate a meeting to discuss the importance of education reform and include material supporting both sides of the issues. By discussing the diverse viewpoints, you will begin to set a context for organizing your own school improvement work. Be sure to include data regarding the local issue you are working on to improve and the research that might be useful to support the discussions.

2

Using Knowledge to Build Organizational Capacity

For almost 50 years, education commissions, reports on school reform, and a host of other education activities called for rigorous academic standards, assessments aligned to those standards, and holding educators accountable for results on raising student achievement and improving teacher quality. Nonetheless, educators still seemed in somewhat of a dilemma regarding what they should do and how they should do it. I experienced that dilemma when I served as president of the First in the World Consortium, a group of local school districts that were the first to take the Third International Mathematics and Science Study (TIMSS). TIMSS is an international assessment of student achievement and teaching in mathematics and science in grades 4, 8, and 12. Despite the fact that the consortium districts were recognized for their high student achievement and located in high socioeconomic communities, it still needed considerable technical and research support from the U.S. Department of Education and the North Central Regional Education Laboratory to process the thousands of pages of data that provided the knowledge on how to improve our mathematics and science programs. We quickly learned that international assessment is a complex task, and that most local school districts simply do not have the resources or capacity to deal with the technical information and data derived from participating in it.

Although the No Child Left Behind Act (NCLB) frequently refers to scientifically based research, there is very little of that type of research available to inform practitioners regarding what products, programs, practices, and policies they should use for their school improvement initiatives. Also, the federal government's effort to provide that type of information through the What Works Clearinghouse is in its embryonic stage. It will take time for the clearinghouse to provide enough research on the required curricular subjects, instructional practices, programs, and policies to help educators who are facing sanctions for not successfully meeting the requirements of NCLB with solutions. When fully operational, the clearinghouse will provide educators with research-based interventions that can be replicated. Currently, however, educators are left with the task of finding the very best evidence- or research-based information to guide their school improvement work. That is a challenging task.

In addition, there is also the task of trying to synthesize the incredible amount of education literature, research studies, product advertisements, and consultant proclamations on how to successfully implement new school initiatives that will work. In other words, trying to sort the valid information from the many resources filled with false and unfounded claims is very difficult for busy practitioners—something akin to separating the wheat from the chaff. This is true especially for teachers who are attempting to implement programs and strategies in their classrooms that will work rather than revert to the ideologically driven learning that is often spurred on by fads and unproven trends.

There is also the contentious debate in the education community about whether some provisions in NCLB, such as using one test to determine adequate yearly progress (AYP) (the 100% success goal for all subgroups of students), and whether the rules for highly qualified teachers are even appropriate. Experience over time, however, has demonstrated that knowledge gained about the performance of the students using NCLB data and the increased requirements for the qualifications of teachers has led to more meaningful discussion regarding their importance and relevance. Arguably, the debate regarding NCLB among educators, policy-makers, and others interested in education continues and, occasionally, consumes more time and energy than what should be the effort to improve the achievement of all students. On one side are the critics of the law who continue to propose corrective actions, and on the other side are the advocates who do not want to make any changes to it. The fact is that NCLB is a federal law, and it is not a simple process to undertake making changes to it. Furthermore, the law is based on using evidence to support program implementation. It incorporates the two critically important tasks for knowledge acquisition—using data and research. If NCLB remains on what is a traditional schedule for reauthorization by Congress, usually every 5 years, it will be 2007 before it receives serious consideration for changes. By then, there will be sufficient data and evidence based on actual case studies and research to support some of the proposed changes currently being discussed by a number of leading educators. In the meantime, the U.S. Department of Education can oversee implementation through the rules and regulations process pertaining to the implementation of the law.

We are spending too much time debating the law and not nearly enough time working on building the capacity in states and local school districts to implement it. NCLB represents a national framework for school improvement. It sets a context for building organizational capacity using knowledge acquisition, knowledge management, and knowledge implementation. On a positive note, however, more discussion in education meetings now focuses on using data and research and offering high-quality professional development. Although it is not a perfect law, rarely are there arguments asserting that its fundamental underpinnings are flawed. Most people believe it is important for all students to receive a high-quality education that is based on specific student learning benchmarks from teachers who are qualified to teach the subjects they are assigned. The "devil is in the details," and currently NCLB should be used as a framework for school improvement and, at some point, the problematic details will be corrected.

As noted in Chapter 1, NCLB represents an educational evolution that occurred during more than four decades in the United States. It led to a national policy calling for rigorous academic standards, assessments aligned to those standards, benchmarks that hold educators accountable for student achievement, and for all teachers to be highly qualified. In the end, if a school district does not have teachers who understand the subject content of what they are assigned to teach and how to teach it, the whole process of sanctions under NCLB becomes a moot issue. It seems intuitive that school improvement efforts should fall under "how to improve a school organization's performance" and let the recommended corrections to the sanction provisions get resolved during the next reauthorization process. The whole concept of building organizational capacity to implement NCLB is analogous to thinking sports teams can win championships without talented athletes and coaches. Without talented teachers, it is not likely that schools can succeed either. Those talented teachers can lead schools to successful NCLB compliance.

To build the organizational capacity of school districts will necessitate breaking the traditional cultural bureaucratic model of school organizations and incorporating more contemporary thinking used in organizations that focus their work around teams. In education, that process calls for using teacher leaders who are trained for their leadership responsibilities and given authority to make decisions to complete their work. That means breaking from the traditional idea that school administration is a line authority process beginning with the superintendent and going down the organizational ladder with assistant superintendents, principals, assistant principals, department chairs, and so on.

This work will also require thinking differently about ways to reconfigure what happens in unsuccessful schools. Successful schools do not have to undergo massive change, but under the provisions of NCLB, in which student achievement data are disaggregated by subgroups, preliminary evidence from even these schools indicates that some groups of students do not do well. This fact was illuminated in our work in the First in the World Consortium. We learned that even in our highest achieving schools, some students were not performing as well as we had hoped. Consequently, it will be important even for schools that are considered highly successful to focus on improving the achievement of all students.

What Is Knowledge?

Having participated in many discussions about knowledge, it has become clear to me that trying to settle on a consensus definition would be counterproductive to the purpose of this book. First, I find that the discussions become so esoteric that they are often rendered meaningless if the basic idea is to help practitioners get a definition of what they need to know that will guide their work to build organizational capacity. Second, I have discovered that reaching a consensus may take too much valuable time from other tasks that have a much higher priority. Parsing definitions of knowledge distracts from the primary task of deciding how you are going to implement the knowledge model to comply with NCLB.

If you define knowledge as familiarity, awareness, or understanding gained through experience or study (American Heritage Dictionary, 1975), then that definition brings together important components of a learning process for a school improvement team. The components incorporate the idea of understanding what needs to be learned using the experience and study of the participants. The "experience" component allows for professional wisdom, and the "study" component uses knowledge gained from data analysis and research reviews. Often, the debate between educators and federal officials is that many teachers believe their professional wisdom has been disregarded and replaced with a one-size-fits-all requirement for using only research-based solutions. The diversity of students in every classroom requires knowledgeable teachers making decisions every day on how to be effective in much the same way a surgeon uses professional wisdom when the standard procedures during an operation are not working. There is no substitute for teacher knowledge and experience as long as it is based on evidence of success.

In *The Knowledge Management Toolkit*, Tiwana (2000) states that knowledge is a "fluid mix of framed experience, values, contextual information, expert insight, and grounded intuition that provides an environment and framework for evaluating new experiences and information" (p. 5). Using Tiwana's definition of knowledge and applying it to school improvement initiatives incorporates the important concept of grounded intuition. As educators confront the challenges of selecting programs and strategies that are intended to raise achievement scores of the most challenging students, it will be important to move past what they have intuitively "thought" worked and implement ideas with evidence that they will work. NCLB is based on results, and there is no time for experimentation before you are confronted with serious sanctions.

With those definitions in mind, as you attempt to build organizational capacity to implement NCLB, the focus needs to be on your familiarity, awareness, and understanding of NCLB's core requirements. In addition, experience and study based on information that is research based or that has demonstrated evidence that a program can work are required. Building that organizational capacity follows a linear process. First, it is essential to acquire the knowledge you need to do the specific school improvement work required by NCLB. Second, you need to manage that knowledge so it does not become so cumbersome that it makes the work too difficult, less likely to be focused, and not result in success. Third, you must use knowledge implementation—the process of professional development—to transfer that knowledge into the actual work of the organization. For education practitioners, that means acquiring the right data and research necessary to identify the work that needs to be done. The process, then, requires researching the right questions and organizing the data and research using a data management process. Finally, the process must be implemented with professional development that is focused, sustained over time, benchmarked to determine progress, led by teachers who are actively involved in the planning and held accountable for results, and guided by research- and evidence-based practices.

Knowledge Implementation Process

- Acquiring the right data and information
- Researching the right questions
- Organizing the data and information
- Implementing the knowledge into the organization

To successfully comply with NCLB will require some difficult decisions about prioritizing curricular offerings and a shift from the traditional culture of schools offering an overly broad range of subjects and services. Many schools do not have the human or capital resources to ensure that all the courses in their curricula are taught by highly qualified teachers as defined in NCLB and that all students achieve proficiency on their state assessments in reading, mathematics, and science. Designating the core subjects defined in NCLB as the focus of the school improvement process could place some subjects at a much lower priority and diminish their quality. NCLB requires accountability for student achievement in reading, mathematics, and science. Designating where school improvement practitioners use their limited resources (personnel, time, and money) will be a very difficult decision-making process. Arguments have been raised by many educators that courses such as the arts, foreign languages, and physical education that are not "tested" and used to determine AYP may be eliminated from the curriculum. Those arguments are likely to be true in lower achieving schools struggling to meet proficiency standards in their states with limited funds for programs.

Core Subjects in NCLB

- English
- Reading or language arts
- Mathematics
- Science
- Foreign languages
- Civics and government
- Economics
- Arts
- History
- Geography

To be certain, there are other requirements that must be met, but building organizational capacity will necessitate a focus on specific priorities that will consume most of the time and energy that teachers can muster to make the needed improvements. The primary focus of NCLB is student achievement in reading, mathematics, and science and having highly qualified teachers. Science requirements are not as comprehensive as those for reading and mathematics and are not going to lead to the serious sanctions for students who do not reach proficiency as quickly. Therefore, it is only logical to begin with the following top priorities: (a) reading, (b) mathematics, and (c) focusing on ensuring that teachers meet their state guidelines to be highly qualified. Often, schools try to undertake too much, sometimes because of internal or external political pressures, and the results are unsuccessful because there was too much on the plate.

In summary, the use of a knowledge model to build organizational capacity and guide compliance with the requirements of NCLB is a process that could lead to school improvement. Knowledge acquisition, management, and implementation are the three core elements of that process. There is no substitute for having the knowledge needed to create success in the NCLB accountability framework.

3

Knowledge Acquisition

The most critical tasks for knowledge acquisition to build organizational capacity are (a) acquiring and analyzing relevant data and (b) using credible research- or evidence-based information from reliable sources. There are a number of reliable sources, and I offer a few examples for use with the knowledge model (Figure 3.1). The purpose of this book is to help practitioners develop a knowledge framework for their school or district to build organizational capacity to comply with the No Child Left Behind Act (NCLB). It is important for school improvement teams to decide what data, research, technology, and professional development best fit their unique needs.

Analyzing data and using credible research will enable you to make informed decisions about how to improve those aspects of your organizational performance that are deficient. Without that knowledge, the process of improving those deficiencies is unlikely to be very substantial. A case can also be made for using that knowledge to sustain and improve those aspects of the organization that are doing as well or better than expected. It is important

Figure 3.1   Knowledge Acquisition

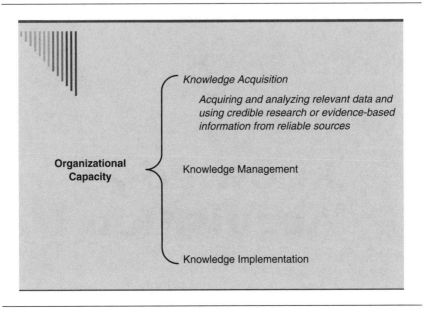

to keep in mind that while working on the deficiencies, it is also essential to sustain what is working well. Sustaining success can be as difficult as the process of improving; just consider how few sports teams repeat as champions or how so many successful businesses lose market share to competitors because they are unable to sustain their success. For example, IBM sold its personal computer division to a Chinese firm in 2004 ("Big Blue's Bold Step," 2004). Not many years ago, even imagining that IBM would not be in the personal computer business would have seemed ludicrous, or, for that matter, that formerly number one Motorola would lag behind a much smaller Sweden-based company, Ericsson, in cellular telephone sales.

Continuous improvement, a concept put forth by W. Edwards Deming, needs to be part of your organizational culture. It is applicable to both the deficient areas in need of improvement and the areas that are successful (Walton, 1991, p. 17). Using data is essential to monitor ongoing progress toward goals.

After using data to identify your performance points, the next step is to conduct a research review and make sense of that research to inform your school improvement planning. It is not necessary to make this task any more complex than necessary. Often, there is a tendency to overload school improvement planning with too many activities and materials, forcing the participants to become overwhelmed and lose their focus on the specific goals. A linear process that begins with (a) acquiring and analyzing specific information (data) that identifies deficiencies and what needs to be accomplished and (b) basing the improvement work on what is learned from credible research on how to implement the process is what is needed.

For example, if a school's reading scores indicate lower than expected student achievement on a state assessment, it makes sense that acquiring relevant data on the areas in which the students are not doing well and reviewing instructional strategy research that informs improvement initiatives are a logical place to begin. Perhaps the student achievement problem is comprehension in the middle grades. The work on reading improvement needs to be focused on the specific topic, comprehension, and then narrowed down using data to fully inform the planning regarding specific comprehension areas in need of improvement. It is important to use an in-depth analysis of the data, determine what types of text comprehension (expository or narrative) are the problem, and then search for other possible comprehension deficiencies. All the research and data analysis should address what is known about comprehension instruction in the middle grades. How is the instruction aligned across departments, grade levels, and courses? Answers to these questions normally can be found in a relatively short period of time. With these answers, you can then organize action items for curricular alignment, implications for instruction, and focus on results that will improve teaching and learning in comprehension.

There is rarely a shortage of data in school districts. As a former superintendent, it was my experience in the school districts I led that both the state and the national testing we did provided teachers with incredible amounts of statistical information about the performance of their students. The problem was that most of the information was never used for a variety of legitimate reasons, the primary one being simply the overwhelming amount of information.

First, nationally normed testing results were returned to the school district in voluminous books filled with data. Very few teachers or principals had the time to process the data, and when they did they spent time on many irrelevant data that distracted from their need to focus on specific issues that should have been identified as "in need of improvement." Much of the data often measured student achievement on tasks or curricula that were not aligned to the district curriculum or state standards. Thus, even with the best of intentions, sincere efforts were undertaken to understand data that did not inform the most critical deficiencies that needed to be addressed. Although nationally normed testing can be used as a benchmark on how students in one school district are doing in comparison to their peers throughout the country, state, or even in their own school district, it often fails to provide the necessary information regarding the specific deficiencies that need to be improved.

Knowing that 22% of your seventh-grade students are reading in the lowest quartile on a nationally normed assessment does not tell you what specifically needs to be done to improve their achievement. Also, although knowing that information is an important starting point, more data are required to enlighten you with regard to the specific deficiencies. That is why state assessments using criterion-referenced testing can be more informative and useful.

With regard to using data, Karen Geenwood Henke (2005) may have said it best when she wrote, "As long as districts need to compile all of this stuff, why not put it to additional use? They're turning data into knowledge and using it in ways they never realized they could" (p. 45).

In *Using Data to Improve Schools* (American Association of School Administrators, n.d.), the authors identify why data are important. Data should be used to

- measure student progress;
- make sure students do not fall through the cracks;
- measure program effectiveness;
- assess instructional effectiveness;
- guide curriculum development;
- allocate resources wisely;
- promote accountability;
- report to the community;
- meet state and federal reporting requirements;
- maintain educational focus; and
- show trends (but not necessarily solutions).

Each of the categories listed in this publication addresses how using data for knowledge acquisition can be applied to school improvement planning; NCLB requires educators to focus on these categories. Only by using relevant data to inform improvement planning will educators achieve their intended results. It is not a good idea to rely on intuition to think you recognize or understand the problems or to provide the solutions. Data provide benchmarks that can demonstrate whether progress is being made.

Building organizational capacity is about acquiring, managing, and implementing knowledge. Acquiring and analyzing data is the starting point. Once you have the data, you have targets on which to focus. School personnel then need to ask why they are getting the current results. Their school improvement plans need to address the answers to the "why?" questions.

Asking "why" is not necessarily an easy task. Tom McGehee (2001), in discussing creation companies, states that

(m)ost organizations forget to ask "why" they are doing what they are doing, and therefore waste a great deal of time, energy, and money. This is accidental, of course. "Why" is not a question encouraged in traditional organizations that ask for obedience first. In creation companies, people learn to ask why before they decide how. (p. 41)

Under NCLB, school districts will be using considerable data from state testing in mathematics, reading, and science. These data provide the starting point for building organizational capacity by acquiring knowledge about student achievement in those subjects. (NCLB also requires states and schools to maintain data on a host of other topics, including the qualifications of teachers and teacher aides, graduation rates, etc.) Information must be gleaned from assessments on how students are performing. The data have multiple components because they are broken down into grade levels and then disaggregated by subgroups, including poverty, race and ethnicity, disability, and limited English proficiency. Once you have the data, the next step should be to organize data retreats with the staff so they fully understand the problems they are dealing with and to collaborate on solutions.

Although, arguably, data retreats could be discussed in more detail in the knowledge implementation chapter of this book, it is more appropriate to describe them here to exemplify how data acquisition and analysis can be used for your improvement planning. The process of building organizational capacity begins with acquiring and analyzing the right information to develop an improvement plan. Data are the cornerstone of focusing on what your current performance status is compared to what it should be. NCLB requires states to implement a formula known as adequate yearly progress (AYP) to ensure that all students are proficient in reading, mathematics, and science by 2014. There has been considerable debate regarding whether this goal is even possible. Although this book is not about that NCLB debate, it should be mentioned here that some of the arguments, such as using longitudinal growth benchmarks for students rather than comparing different groups of students each year by grade level, offer hope that the process of assessment and data use will become more sophisticated in schools over time.

Finally, all AYP formulas are written by the states and not the federal government. Whereas some states have taken the responsibility seriously and set challenging goals for their schools, others have chosen to develop less rigorous goals to look good statistically.

In the end, NCLB has a check and balance provision (e.g., requiring states to participate in the National Assessment of Education Progress, a national assessment measuring the achievement of U.S. students in a variety of subjects and grade levels) that will illuminate results from those states whose standards may not be rigorous enough.

Data Retreats

The data retreat is a substantive planning process that enables school improvement teams to focus on their priorities. It is one of the two critical tasks for acquiring knowledge to build organizational capacity.

Learning Point Associates, a nonprofit educational organization empowering educators to transform student learning, offers a specialized data retreat program for schools or school districts (Learning Point Associates, 2001). The data retreats are intended to lead teams of teachers through reflective collaboration and analysis of their school's data. Understanding and analyzing data is critical to undertaking a school improvement initiative. It provides knowledge about how the district or school or both are performing compared to their goals as well as insight into short- and long-term trends.

The Learning Point Associates data retreat is organized into eight steps:

1. Developing leadership teams, setting the context, and organizing the data retreat

2. Collecting and organizing the data

3. Analyzing data patterns

4. Posing hypotheses

5. Developing improvement goals

6. Designing specific strategies

7. Defining evaluation criteria

8. Making the commitment

In Step 1, leadership plays an important role. I noted previously that as a former superintendent, I brought too much data to the process and did not focus on what might have been the district's most critical deficiencies. It cannot be overstated here that it is essential to collect the right data. In *Good to Great*, Jim Collins (2001, p. 88) notes that all good to great companies "began the process of finding a path to greatness by confronting the brutal facts of their current reality." He goes on to say that truth is heard in four basic practices:

1. Lead with questions, not answers.

2. Engage in dialogue and debate, not coercion.

3. Conduct autopsies, without blame.

4. Build red flag mechanisms that turn information into information that cannot be ignored.

I equate Collins's statement to what I call a possum theory: Unless you poke it, you will not know whether it is dead or alive. Poking your data can stimulate thought-provoking discussions among faculty regarding how you can improve your student achievement, but you must have the data to organize a meaningful discussion.

Because the data retreat is about knowledge acquisition, it is important to enlist the work of a diverse group of specialists to help process the information. Although it is recommended that the team not exceed seven members, the members should have backgrounds in the core subjects and represent the grade spans being reviewed. Because testing under NCLB is required in grades 3 through 8, once in high school, teachers, administrators (particularly building level), and assessment and curriculum specialists from these grade levels should be represented on the team. Additional consideration should be given to having representatives from special education and English as a Second Language staff actively involved with the team because they are integral to meeting the requirements of NCLB.

Be cognizant of the fact that a team of teachers and administrators will not take their assignment seriously if time is not devoted to explaining why a data retreat team has been organized and what the team is expected to do. It is critical for all members of the team to recognize the importance of collecting, understanding, and using data to inform their NCLB compliance work. State testing under NCLB sets an important context for this work, and obviously the sanctions associated with not meeting the AYP goals of the law provide an incentive to carefully review the data.

School Sanctions Under NCLB for Not Meeting AYP

- After 2 years—receive technical assistance, develop school improvement plan, and offer public school choice
- After 3 years—must provide students with supplemental services
- After 4 years—a corrective action plan, including replacement of some staff, new curriculum, and professional development
- After 5 years—change school governance structure, which may include state takeover, private contractor, and staff restructuring or converting to a charter school

Step 2 of the data retreat is collecting and organizing the data. It is during this step that the process can become overwhelming. The primary focus in this step is on student achievement data, but NCLB requires other data to be maintained, including resource allocations and personnel information regarding highly qualified teachers and aides. In most instances, monitoring data other than student achievement will be handled by other departments in the school district.

For NCLB, it is essential to use the state assessment data to meet minimum proficiency requirements, but schools do not need only try to meet the basic requirements of the law. The best schools will look beyond the basic requirements and core subjects to ensure high quality throughout all their programs. The caveat, however, is that you must first be doing well in the core subjects before you can take on the additional work. It is analogous to when a student who is doing poorly in class asks if he or she can do some extra credit work when his or her attention should be focused on the regular class assignments.

There are numerous other data sources that can be used to inform school improvement, including the major nationally normed testing services, student achievement through grade cards and portfolios, student demographic patterns, course offerings, and how resources are being used to fund various programs.

In Step 2, you need to frame your questions carefully and be certain they are focused on the right issues. The following are examples of questions to ask:

- What longitudinal patterns do we have regarding our student achievement in each core subject identified in NCLB?
- What is the student achievement in each of the core subjects for all the required subgroups?
- How can we be sure that our data are reliable? Can we be certain the scores are accurate and valid, and do the scores measure what they were intended to measure?
- How many of our teachers will need support to comply with the highly qualified teacher provisions?
- How can we allocate resources to support the priorities we establish?

Finding the data to answer these questions is the beginning of the process to build your organizational capacity to address them. Also, it may be a good idea to remember what Jim Collins said regarding how important it is to know the brutal facts of current reality.

Step 3 of Learning Point Associates's data retreats is to analyze the data using a quadnocular view identifying achievement, perception, program, and demographic patterns. The purpose of a quadnocular view is to uncover patterns and relationships among the data that will provide a focus for the school improvement plan. This process is driven by the data retreat team using collaboration, observation, and reflection to "mine" the data.

Although time-consuming and labor-intensive, analyzing data is critical to successfully complying with NCLB. It is a scientific process that is focused and guided by specific benchmarks. Under NCLB, some schools that were previously identified as being excellent had the reporting advantage of averaging their test scores. Thus, a school with a predominantly high-achieving student population may have had a large percentage of students achieving proficiency on its state assessment tests, but the small percentage of students not meeting proficiency was generally the same subgroup of students year in and year out. The requirement in NCLB to disaggregate data by poverty, race and ethnicity, disability, and limited English proficiency prevents these schools from camouflaging their subgroup achievement scores and not addressing a consistently underperforming group of students. More important, it does not mean these are not excellent schools. Having the knowledge from the data required by NCLB forces them to confront the achievement deficiencies of these students and ensure high-quality performance throughout the entire organization. It prevents complacency even when student achievement scores are very good.

After the first three steps are completed, data retreat Step 4 involves posing hypotheses. A hypothesis is nothing more than a theory or explanation for what you believe is the reason for the patterns and achievement scores. Hypotheses are not proven statements of fact but incorporate the professional wisdom of the data retreat team as to possible causes of what you have learned.

You might pose certain questions. For example, why does one subgroup of students outperform another subgroup in fifth-grade reading but not in sixth-grade reading if that is an observed achievement pattern? Why don't our students perform better in mathematics in the primary grades? Why is our graduation rate lower than those of neighboring schools? These types of questions can lead to posing relevant hypotheses that will guide the acquisition of research knowledge to build the capacity of the organization to solve its problems. In the end, you will ultimately accept or reject your hypotheses based on the data analysis in Step 3 and your research.

In Step 5 of the data retreat, you develop your improvement goals. After reviewing your data and analyzing patterns, you have the information needed to determine your goals. The goals should be both short and long term. NCLB's requirement that states set a formula for AYP is a daunting challenge to many schools. For some schools, there is what is known as a safe harbor provision. Safe harbor enables schools that do not make AYP but reduce the number of nonproficient students in any subgroup by 10% in a single year as making AYP. Safe harbor could be a short-term goal to help those schools begin the process of successful school improvement. John Kotter, mentioned previously, cites short-term wins as one of the eight critical steps in the change process. He explains that short-term wins "nourish faith in the change effort" (Kotter & Cohen, 2002, p. 125). Schools that have had consistently high percentages of students not achieving proficiency could set attainable goals using the safe harbor provision. Also, successfully attaining those goals could lead to a positive culture change in the organization and, ultimately, significant improvement.

In Step 6, the team designs specific strategies that lead to improving the deficiencies and meeting the improvement goals set in Step 5. Included in this step is a review of the strategies currently used and discussion of strategies that have proven effective in improving student achievement and teaching in those areas identified as in need of improvement. The goals need to be meaningful and supported by a total commitment from the organization. NCLB requires specific achievement targets, and as noted previously, the sanctions for not meeting those targets can be very serious. As your goals are written, it is imperative to maintain a laser-like focus on the data and research being used to achieve them. The district must use programs, products, practices, and policies that are proven to work. At this step of the school improvement process, it is not worthwhile to jump on a fad bandwagon, an unproven practice used frequently in education.

Defining evaluation criteria, often a neglected aspect of the school improvement process, is Step 7 of the data retreat. This step involves determining your progress to date and assessing if you have successfully accomplished your goals. Often, evaluation is not integrated into the school improvement plan. Ideally, evaluation should be conducted on two levels. First, there should be a plan developed to analyze the effectiveness of the strategies selected by the team. As achievement data are generated relative to those strategies, the team should review the data to determine if there are patterns of success or failure over time. Do not jump to hasty conclusions; give the strategies a reasonable time period to determine if they work. Second, the evaluation plan should enable the team to determine what progress, if any, was made toward achieving the targeted goals. Only through an unbiased evaluation will the team be able to build on its work and strive for continuous improvement. If funds are limited, it is possible to conduct your own evaluation, but the evaluation must be based on very specific criteria spelled out in Step 7. If funding is available, a more appropriate evaluation should be contracted out to an external evaluator, one who is not an employee of the organization. External evaluation can prevent conflicts of interest or "spinning" of the results.

Finally, data retreat Step 8 is about making the commitment to sustain the effort. Do not be misled, however; the process of a data retreat does not begin and end with these eight steps. To build organizational capacity, it is essential to maintain the data analysis work on an ongoing basis. Kotter and Cohen (2002, p. 161) cite making changes stick as the eighth step in the change process. It is not uncommon for school improvement plans to be implemented and then dissolve into the pile of efforts that were undertaken in the past only to not be sustained.

The framework that NCLB sets for a school improvement model is logical, and the data it requires focus on continuous improvement. Those data provide essential knowledge about whether the district or school is meeting its goals. A data retreat will enable school improvement teams to acquire and analyze relevant data to inform their work.

Using Credible Research- or Evidence-Based Information or Both

The second of the two most critical tasks for knowledge acquisition to build organizational capacity is using credible research- or evidence-based information from reliable sources. Although this may sound easy, the amount of literature in education is so voluminous that it is unreasonable to expect teachers and administrators to find the time to sift through it and find the high-quality research that is likely to help them with their work. Complicating the process is that there is often conflicting research with conclusions that support or reject various interventions. More bluntly, finding education research that meets reasonable scientific research standards can be like searching for the proverbial needle in a haystack.

Educators have long been susceptible to education fads or have passionately advocated for curricular programs based on their ideologies about what they believe will work in schools and classrooms. The 1980s and 1990s produced some very intense ideological debates in reading and mathematics. During the 1980s, there was intense debate over whole language or phonics instruction in reading. In the 1990s, the debate was about computation versus conceptual understanding of mathematical processes. What was often absent from these debates was scientific research supporting either side's arguments with evidence demonstrating how these instructional practices could improve the quality of learning for all students. From my perspective, these debates did more harm than good because they detracted from the primary purpose of teaching, which is to ensure that all students are successful in their classes. Too much time was devoted to the debate and not nearly enough time to finding research-based answers regarding how those programs worked in the multitude of environments of urban, suburban, and rural classrooms. Interestingly, most of the debates diminished when both sides realized each had some valid points.

Another problem is the number of fad bandwagons that educators jump on. In the 1970s, educators thought open classrooms would work. Many schools went through the costly process of knocking out walls only to discover not only that they were not the answer to improving schools but also that the noise levels in them were often intolerable for both students and teachers. I remember early in my career the accolades given to educational television: Using television technology was going to help every teacher be more successful. It was not unusual for school districts to go to the expense of funding a TV for each classroom only to later discover that the TVs were not being used. Recently, teachers are hearing about brain research. Perhaps brain research is a topic that will ultimately help them improve their teaching and student achievement, but there is no evidence that teachers need to spend valuable professional development time on it at the expense of not being involved in more content knowledge and instructional strategy activities that would likely yield better results. About fads, Gail Russell Chaddock (1998) says that teachers call it the "reform de jour," and for many, it is the "biggest challenge at the start of any school year. That's when the latest idea for how to improve student performance kicks in." Implementing fads that are unproven is not unusual in schools.

The No Child Left Behind Act has created more concern among educators about using education research to inform their decision making as a result of more than 100 references to scientifically based research in the law, which NCLB defines as "research that involves the application of rigorous, systematic, and objective procedures to obtain reliable and valid knowledge relevant to education activities and programs." Following passage of NCLB, Congress reauthorized the Office of Education Research and Improvement into the Institute of Education Sciences (IES) through the Education Sciences and Reform Act of 2002. IES was established to expand knowledge and provide information on the condition of education, practices that improve academic achievement, and the effectiveness of federal and other education programs. The formal description of the IES mission aligns closely with the basic concept of this book: "the transformation of education into an evidence-based field in which decision makers routinely seek out the best available research and data before adopting programs or practices that will affect significant number of students" (www.ed.gov/about/ offices/list/ies/index.html). IES is organized into three centers: the National Center for Education Statistics, the National Center for Education Research, and the National Center for Evaluation and Regional Assistance.

IES will not, and from a practical perspective cannot, be the only source of research or evidence to use when making critical decisions about programs, products, practices, and policies. School improvement teams and school leaders will need to gather additional information to support their work. Caution must be used when reviewing that information. There is considerable education research available, but determining which research is useful can be a daunting challenge. Also, not all the research is scientifically based, meaning that it may be necessary to make critical school improvement decisions based on the information that is available. There are numerous case studies, surveys, and action research projects that can be very tempting to use to support your work. You might want to ask the following, however:

- Were they conducted in an environment that is very similar to the one in which you plan to implement the new program?
- Do they address the specific objectives you have for the new program?
- Were the conditions where the study was conducted almost exactly the same as yours?

Most likely, it will not be useful to use an action research study from an urban classroom to support a new program you want to implement in a rural setting. All educational practitioners need to be informed critical consumers of the research, evidence, and literature they use to improve programs to meet the specific benchmarks contained in NCLB.

Setting a Context for Education Research: The National Research Council Committees

The National Research Council has undertaken the responsibility of sponsoring two reports on recommendations for scientific principles in education research and advancing scientific research in education. These reports are important because they set a context for how broad-based education research should be planned and provide vital suggestions for making that research applicable to school improvement efforts.

The recommendations for the guiding principles from the first report, *Scientific Research in Education* (Shavelson & Towne, 2002), are to

- pose significant questions that can be investigated empirically;
- link research to relevant theory;
- use methods that permit direct investigation of the question;
- provide a coherent and explicit chain of reasoning;
- replicate and generalize across studies; and
- disclose research to professional scrutiny and critique.

The second report, *Advancing Scientific Research in Education* (Towne, Wise, & Winters, 2005), was the result of work by a committee that was convened to discuss how education research could be improved. This report offered recommendations in three basic categories—promoting quality, building the knowledge base, and enhancing professional development. The following are the recommendations with the most significance for practitioners:

- Federal agencies should ensure appropriate resources are available for education researchers conducting large-scale investigations in educational settings to build partnerships with practitioners and policymakers.
- Professional associations and education research journals should work in concert with funding agencies to create an infrastructure that takes advantage of technology to facilitate

data sharing and knowledge accumulation in education research.

- Education research journals should develop and implement policies to require structured abstracts.
- Schools of education that train doctoral students for careers in education research should provide those students with a variety of meaningful research experiences.

The National Research Council reports set a critical first-step context for improving education research. Without relevant research conducted on practical issues that confront teachers and administrators struggling to implement NCLB, many more years of educational decision mistakes will be repeated. Research that can be used by practitioners to truly improve teaching and learning could be a significant transformation in education.

U.S. Department of Education Research Initiative

The task of using scientifically based research, as required by NCLB, will take time, but there needs to be a starting point. Knowledge acquisition for school improvement needs to be used now. It is important for education researchers to implement the principles and recommendations from the National Research Council quickly. Knowing more about the principles and results from research will help school improvement teams inform their knowledge acquisition work.

The U.S. Department of Education has undertaken a significant project to help educators overcome that burden by establishing the What Works Clearinghouse (WWC) (www.whatworks.ed.gov). As mentioned previously, the clearinghouse will collect, screen, and identify studies of the effectiveness of educational interventions that are defined as programs, products, practices, and policies. Although it will take time to build the database, at the very least educators now have a credible resource that will attempt to ensure that these interventions meet essential criteria before being posted on the WWC Web site. Although not a perfect solution to meeting the needs of school improvement teams, the WWC is the first resource that will hold those who make claims about their programs and services to a standard much higher than selling "elixirs" to schools. Those elixirs often cost more money and consume valuable time with little chance of long-term success.

The WWC posts research findings on its Web site in a user-friendly format. Those findings are the type of research information that has not been readily available to educators. The clearinghouse will review the interventions (i.e., the programs, products, practices, and policies) and hold them to a scientific research standard. It will provide information on credible evaluation studies of the interventions. Educators who use the WWC can have confidence that the claims being made on behalf of the interventions have been reviewed through a process that is not connected to the interventions or the evaluators having anything to gain or lose when publishing the conclusions. It is hoped that the WWC will prevent schools from being led into another fad that does not work.

At numerous professional education meetings, exhibit halls are filled with vendors who claim their products will raise reading or math scores quickly. Rarely do these exhibitors discuss whether these gains will be sustained over time or what research is available to determine if their products will be successful in particular settings. The WWC will enable educators to ask these vendors or consultants whether their interventions have been posted on its Web site.

The WWC reports are intended to support decision making and are not endorsements of products or services by the U.S. Department of Education. The clearinghouse advises educators that no single report should be used as a basis for making policy decisions because (a) few studies are designed and implemented flawlessly and (b) all studies are tested on a limited number of participants, using a limited number of outcomes, and at a limited number of times, so generalizing from one study to any context is difficult. To highlight these issues, the clearinghouse reports describe, in detail, the specifics of each study, focusing primarily on studies that provide the best evidence of effects (randomized controlled trials). Systematic reviews of the evidence will be conducted to summarize the results of the individual studies.

For school improvement teams, reviewing what research is available on the clearinghouse site would be an informative first step for collecting trusted research on a particular topic. The following information was taken directly from the WWC Web site as an example of what you will see when using it. In math, there are five programs that have been reviewed, including WWC's review of the Saxon Math program. The Saxon study can be used to demonstrate how using the clearinghouse site may help educators involved in a math study acquire knowledge about Saxon Math that is research based. The clearinghouse's study is not an endorsement of the program; rather, it demonstrates the types of information and questions that are essential when participating in a mathematics curriculum review that are available on the WWC Web site. Reflecting on the highly controversial math curriculum debates of the 1990s, having the clearinghouse studies would have been helpful to many educators who were criticized for their program decisions.

For example, the only study that meets evidence standards found that there was no significant difference in posttest scores between the Saxon Math students and the comparison group. That information would have been helpful to educators who were criticized for selecting programs that used a different approach to mathematics instruction. Also, the source for the information was trusted and derived from a research study that met high standards. It is important to also note, however, that WWC warns that using the results from one study can be unreliable for decision making. For this reason, there are other studies on the site that the school improvement team could use to support its work.

Figure 3.2 provides an overview of the intervention report. Figure 3.3 is a profile of Saxon Math and includes information on the teaching strategies, scope of use, and the cost of the program. In Figure 3.4, the information about the study is provided. The slide notes that one of the two studies was a randomized controlled trial and the other a quasi-experimental design. Figure 3.5 includes references and a table showing the differences between the Saxon students and the

Figure 3.2   WWC intervention report on the Saxon Math study

What Works Clearinghouse

Institute of Education Sciences

Curriculum-based interventions for increasing K-12 math achievement—middle school

Intervention report	Saxon Math	Updated December 1, 2004

Intervention	*Saxon Math* curricula and materials are available for grades K through 12, with the content and skills designed to meet National Council of Teachers of Mathematics (NCTM) and various state standards. Each course lasts for one year, and students participate in 120-lesson courseware packages that last for about 60 minutes a day. Used in teacher-led lessons, *Saxon Math* is designed to teach in increments, provide continual practice, and test cumulative learning every five lessons.
For	Middle school students.
Findings	One randomized controlled trial on *Saxon Math* found no significant difference in posttest scores between students using *Saxon Math* and the comparison group using the University of Chicago Mathematics Project NCTM curriculum. One quasi-experimental design study found that students using *Saxon Math* had higher gains in overall math, math computation, and math concepts compared with other students. However, the study analyzed the data at the wrong level, making it impossible to accurately determine the significance of the finding.
Evidence base	✔ 1 randomized controlled trial meets evidence standards.
	✔ 1 quasi-experimental design study meets evidence standards with reservations.
	✖ 4 studies do not meet evidence screens. *(see symbol key on page 7)*
Evidence limits	The evidence base is limited to two studies. The first is a randomized controlled trial of 6th-grade students in a rural-suburban Nebraska junior high school. A second study is a quasi-experimental design study of 8th-grade students in Oklahoma City middle schools. Quasi-experimental studies provide weaker evidence of effects because it is possible that unmeasured differences between the groups affected the findings. Further, this study analyzed the data at the wrong level, which may bias the findings. The samples for both studies were small (36–78 students). Four studies do not meet evidence standards.
Scope of use	*Saxon Math's* first textbook (Algebra 1 for 9th grade) was implemented in 1980, and *Saxon Algebra 1/2* (6th grade) was implemented in 1986. Information is not available about the number and demographics of students, schools, or districts using the intervention.
Developer and contact	Saxon Publishers, www.saxonpublishers.com; email: info@saxonpublishers.com; telephone: (800) 284–7019.

WWC Intervention Reports   1

SOURCE: Reproduced with permission from the U.S. Department of Education.

comparison group. The Appendix slide, Figure 3.6, includes summary information contained in the tables. Finally, in Figure 3.7, the characteristics of interventions for the Saxon Math study are described.

Having this type of information on curricular programs could be a significant part of the report containing recommendations for new programs that school improvement teams make to their boards of education. Their recommendations would be supported by independent research rather than claims made by vendors or others whose primary interest is the sale of their products or services. There will be more programs to select from in the future to offer the school improvement teams options to meet their unique local needs. The WWC information will give educators confidence that their recommendations have credible research supporting them. It is analogous to the situation in which a doctor prescribes a

Figure 3.3 WWC profile of the Saxon Math study

Profile *Saxon Math* focuses on fundamental mathematics skills, targeting children from kindergarten through grade 12. This report focuses on middle school math, defined as grades 6 through 9. The 6th grade curriculum covers simplifying expressions containing parentheses, graphing functions, and understanding ratios and proportions. The 7th grade curriculum covers pre-algebra topics such as rate, powers, roots, and geometric proofs. The 8th grade curriculum covers all topics usually taught in pre-algebra in addition to topics from geometry and discrete mathematics. The 9th grade curriculum covers all topics usually taught in a first-year algebra course (such as exponents, roots, and algebraic word problems) as well as conceptual understanding, procedural fluency, strategic competence, adaptive reasoning, and productive disposition. As stated by the developers, *Saxon Math* covers all five content and skill areas of NCTM standards and meets various state standards.

Teaching
Each grade of *Saxon Math* consists of 120 daily lessons and 12 activity-based investigations. A daily lesson consists of warm-up (10–15 minutes), introduction to the new concept (5–10 minutes), practice focusing on new concept (5 minutes), and mixed practice focusing on new and previously learned concepts (20–30 minutes). Students are introduced to concepts incrementally, given opportunities of continual review and practice, and assessed cumulatively and frequently (every fifth lesson). An assessment score of 80% or lower indicates a need for remediation, and a provision for remediation is part of the program.

Lessons are designed to be one hour daily (this includes practice and review time), and assessments occur every fifty lesson, usually on Friday each week.

The teacher is responsible for facilitating and mediating the warm-up session, introducing the new concept, and conducting the practice sessions. Teachers introduce the daily concept using manipulatives or representative models accompanied by the procedures needed to solve the problem. Teachers are instructed to conduct lessons in sequence, not skip lessons, limit direct instruction to 10–15 minutes of group (or individual) instruction, spend the majority of class time allowing children to do mathematics problems in the problem sets, and assign all problems in each set.

Supports are available for teachers of *Saxon Math*. Each state has an educational representative. The curriculum developers have a comprehensive Web site offering general information, resource materials, and an email address for questions. Other supports include customer service representatives, in-service training, telephone teacher support, a helpline, teachers' resource booklets, in-service videos, and administrator's guides to help principals and administrators implement *Saxon Math* in their classrooms.

Scope of use
Saxon Math's first textbook (Algebra 1 for 9th grade) was implemented in 1960 and *Saxon Algebra* 1/2 (8th grade) was implemented in 1968. Information about the number and demographics of students, schools, or districts currently using the intervention is not available from the Web site or the customer service or educational representatives.

Cost
The student text costs approximately $50. Additional materials, including the teacher's manual, can total approximately $360–$900 more.

WWC Intervention Reports 2

SOURCE: Reproduced with permission from the U.S. Department of Education.

particular medicine from a variety of choices knowing that each medicine passed a clinical trial and has worked when treating specific illnesses. The WWC has that same potential for educators. It will be important for the clearinghouse to adhere to high ethical and guiding principles for its work rather than ideological beliefs. If it does, it will enhance the decisions that school improvement teams make regarding interventions.

Using the Research Knowledge

Once you have the data and have identified the problems that need to be corrected to be in compliance with NCLB, small, specialized learning communities, composed primarily of teachers, can begin

Figure 3.4   Information about the Saxon Math study

Study findings	*Randomized controlled trial*	*Quasi-experimental design*
	The single randomized controlled trial on *Saxon Math* (Peters 1992) found no significant difference in posttest scores between students in *Saxon Math* and the comparison group when controlling on pretest. The intervention group scored slightly but not significantly higher than the comparison group. There was no evidence that the *Saxon Math* intervention was more or less effective than the comparison curriculum, the University of Chicago Mathematics Project NCTM curriculum.	The single quasi-experimental design study on *Saxon Math* (Crawford & Raia 1986) found that students in the intervention group made significant gains in overall math and math computation scores but not on math concepts scores, compared with the comparison group. Because of the limitations in the way the analysis was conducted, it is not possible to determine whether these findings are due to the curriculum or to chance.
Strength of the evidence base	The WWC collected more than 800 studies for the Middle School Math Curriculum review. Six looked at the effects of *Saxon Math*. One study, a small randomized controlled trial without serious problems, met WWC evidence standards. A second study, a small quasi-experimental design study without serious problems, met WWC evidence standards with reservations. The remaining four studies did not meet WWC evidence screens. In three of these studies, there was only one intervention and one comparison unit, so the analysis could not separate the effects of the intervention from other factors. The fourth study, a quasi-experimental design study, does not account for pre-existing differences between groups with matching or equating. Studies were rated according to the strength of their causal evidence. Studies that placed students into the intervention and comparison groups randomly (randomized controlled trials) without notable design or implementation flaws are classified as meeting evidence standards (✐). Other studies that use comparison groups (quasi-experimental designs) and randomized control trials with notable flaws are classified as meeting evidence standards with reservations (✐[a]).	Studies are further rated for intervention fidelity, outcome measures, breadth of evidence, reporting on subgroups, analysis, and statistical reporting. That information is provided in study reports, but does not affect the overall rating. In both studies, the interventions were well designed and implemented—and both studies used nationally normed, standardized tests. Neither study looked at all important groups of students or settings. There were several issues with the analysis. The studies were small—the randomized controlled trial had 36 students and the quasi-experimental design study had 78 students. Further, some students in the RCT switched groups, and findings from the QED study should be viewed with caution because of problems with the analysis. Tables A3–A4 describe the outcome studies conducted on *Saxon Math* that meet WWC evidence standards and meet WWC evidence standards with reservations. For a more detailed description of the study, *see* the <u>*Detailed study Reports*</u> or <u>*Brief Study Reports*</u>. a See symbol key on page 7.
References	✐ Peters, K. G. (1992). *Skill performance comparability of two algebra programs on an eighth-grade population.* Unpublished doctoral dissertation. University of Nebraska, Lincoln. ✐ Crawford, J., & Raia, F. (1986, February). *Analyses of eighth grade math texts and achievement (evaluation report).* Oklahoma City: Planning, Research, and Evaluation Department, Oklahoma City Public Schools.	⊗ Clay, D. W. (1996). *A study to determine the effects of a non-traditional approach to algebra instruction on student achievement.* Master's thesis, Salem-Teikyo University. (ERIC Document Reproduction Service No. ED428963) ⊗ Lafferty, J. F. (1996). The links among mathematics text, students' achievement, and students' mathematics anxiety: A comparison of the incremental development and traditional.

WWC Intervention Reports   3

SOURCE: Reproduced with permission from the U.S. Department of Education.

considering how research can inform their work. The idea of forming learning communities should not be taken lightly. Peter Senge (1990) is recognized for his work in this area. His model should be considered with a serious approach to school improvement planning. Senge describes five disciplines of systems thinking:

- Systems Thinking—a process to help identify patterns and learn to reinforce or change them effectively
- Personal Mastery—a high level of proficiency to bring about desired results
- Mental Models—understanding and taking action based on notions and assumptions that may reside deeply in the psyche

Figure 3.5　　Differences between Saxon Math students and the comparison group

References
(continued)

texts. *Dissertation Abstracts International, 56* (06), 3014A (UMI No. 9537065)

⊘ Rentsochler, R.V. (1994). The effects of Saxon's incremental review on computational skills and problem-solving achievement of

sixth-grade students. *Dissertation Abstracts International, 56* (02), 464A. (UMI No. 9516017)

⊗ Saxon, J. (1982). Incremental development: A breakthrough in mathematics. *Phi Delta kappan, 63* (4), 482–484.

Table 1
Effects

The *Saxon Math* group seemed to score better than the comparison group, but the difference is not significant. For the randomized controlled trial, we are 95% confident that the

difference between the two groups was somewhere between –0.54 (favoring the comparison group) and 0.76 (favoring the *Saxon Math* group).

Study	Measure	Favors comparison group –2.00	–1.50	–1.00	–0.50	Comparison group mean 0	0.50	1.00	Favors Saxon Math group 1.50	2.00
⊘ Peters 1992	Orleans-Hanna Algebra PrognosisTest[a] (N=36 students)					0.11				
⊘ Crawford & Rala 1986	CAT Overall Math[b] (N=78 students[c])					0.41[d]				
	CAT Math Concepts[b] (N=78 students[c])					0.28[d]				
	CAT Math Computation[b] (N=78 students[c])					0.44[d]				
Approximate percentile ranking		**2%**	**7%**	**16%**	**31%**	**50%**	**69%**	**84%**	**93%**	**98%**

a A nationally normed, standardized test.
b California Achievement Test, a nationally normed, standardized test.
c Sample size reported is unit of analysis, not unit of assignment.
d When there is no solid line, the study did not provide data to correctly compute the confidence interval.
How to read this table: The wide, shaded bar indicates both the direction and estimated size of the effect of the intervention. The estimated effects reported here are standardized differences in the mean values between the intervention and comparison groups. Bars extending to the right of zero denote estimated effects that favor the intervention group and those extending to the left of zero denote estimated effects that favor the comparison group. The solid line through the shaded bar marks the 95% confidence interval of the estimated effect. When the line does not cross zero (and the bar is solid, not striped), the estimate is statistically significant. The bar is striped if the effect is not significant or if significance could not be accurately computed. The scale at the bottom of the chart indicates the approximate percentile distribution of students in the control group. The percentile ranking at the end of the shaded bar can be used to interpret the standardized mean difference in the outcome. For example, an effect of .5 is roughly equivalent to an increase in the mean value from that of the average student in the comparison group (50th percentile) to that of the average student at the 69th percentile.

What Works Clearinghouse　　The What Works Clearinghouse (www.whatworks.ed.gov) was established in 2002 by the U.S. Department of Education's Institute of Education Sciences to provide educators, policymakers, researchers, and the public with a central and trusted source of scientific evidence of what works in education. Please email all questions and comments to Info@whatworks.ed.gov. The What Works Clearinghouse is administered by the U.S. Department of Education through a contract to a joint venture of the American Institutes for Research and the Campbell Collaboration.　　　4

SOURCE: Reproduced with permission from the U.S. Department of Education.

- Shared Vision—an organization's goals, values, and mission being shared
- Team Learning—when members suspend assumptions and think together to solve problems and chart the future

Senge has been quoted as saying that new insights fail to get into practice because they conflict with deeply held images of how the world works. As is well-known, people are often reluctant to change. The accountability provisions of NCLB, however, have demonstrated the difficult challenge the federal government faces when legislating a national policy for all the states and local school districts that requires significant change.

Figure 3.6   Summary information for the Saxon Math study

Appendix

Table A1   Summary characteristics and findings from randomized controlled trials on *Saxon Math*

Study	Study sample	Measure	Sample size			Mean outcome		Standard deviation[a]		Estimated Impact[b]	
			Intervention group	Comparison group	Total	Intervention group	Comparison group	Intervention group	Comparison group	Mean difference	Standardized mean difference
Peters 1992	8th grade "math-talented" students	[General] achievement test[c]	19	17	36 students	95.6	95.1	4.53	4.09	0.5	0.11 (±0.65)

Table A2   Summary characteristics and findings from quasi-experimental design studies on *Saxon Math*

Study	Study sample	Measure	Sample size			Mean outcome		Standard deviation[a]		Estimated Impact[b]	
			Intervention group	Comparison group	Total	Intervention group	Comparison group	Intervention group	Comparison group	Mean difference	Standardized mean difference
Crawford & Rala 1986	8th grade students	CAT[d] Overall Math	39	39	78 students[e]	55.56	50.72	11.86	11.75	4.84	0.41[f]
	8th grade students	CAT[d] Math Concepts	39	39	78 students[e]	53.36	49.82	12.44	12.40	3.54	0.20[f]
	8th grade students	CAT[d] Math Computation	39	39	78 students[e]	57.59	51.51	13.35	14.14	6.08	0.44[f]

a Shows how dispersed the participants' outcomes are. A small deviation would suggest that participants had similar outcomes.
b The WWC computed standardized effects, using reported by the study author.
c A 60-Item nationally normed, standardized test to predict student success in future algebra study.
d California Achievement Test.
e The sample size reported is unit of analysis, not unit of assignment.
f The unit of analysis did not match the unit of assignment, so accurate confidence intervals could not be computed.

SOURCE: Reproduced with permission from the U.S. Department of Education.

Senge's five disciplines form the basis of substantive knowledge work in a small learning community. His approach to learning communities focusing on discussions of education research- and evidence-based information can support a quality school improvement initiative. Using NCLB as a framework, concentrating on research with specialized learning communities in the school or district in reading, mathematics, and science, and working with the data on subgroups could bring a structured focus to implementing successful interventions. In addition, the process allows for open, meaningful dialogue between the participants. Research alone will not be the answer, but when coupled with the professional wisdom of the practitioners, this will offer a significant combination that should lead to successful outcomes.

Figure 3.7   Characteristics of the interventions for the Saxon Math study

Table A3	Characteristics of Interventions in reviewed studies on *Saxon Math:* Peters 1992	
Evidence base rating[a]	**Characteristic**	**Description**
◉	Study citation	Peters, K. G. (1992). *Skill performance comparability of two algebra programs on an eighth-grade population.* Unpublished doctoral dissertation, University of Nebraska, Lincoln, NE.
	Participants	36 8th-grade students. All the students were "math-talented" based on teacher recommendations, prior academic achievement, and personal maturity.
	setting	Junior high school in a rural suburban district abutting Lincoln, Nebraska; students randomly assigned to one of two classrooms (one intervention classroom and one comparison classroom). The same teacher taught both the intervention and comparison groups.
	Intervention	Participants in the Intervention group were taught using the *Saxon Math* curriculum for 8th grade students (Algebra 1/2). Students in this group participated in 60-minute daily sessions for one year. In each session, the teacher introduced a new concept incrementally, and students had opportunities to practice the new concept and past concepts during each session. Students were assessed every fifth lesson. The Intervention is designed to cover 120 lessons in one year.
	Comparison	Participants in the comparison group were taught using an NCTM standards based curriculum called the University of Chicago Mathematics Project designed to: build Independent learners and thinkers, build understanding of math vocabulary (such as mathematical signs), emphasize reviewing concepts within existing lessons, and increase student comprehension.
	Primary outcomes and measurement	The primary outcome measure is the Orleans-Hanna Algebra Prognosis Test, a nationally normed, valid, and reliable 60-item test designed to predict student success in future algebra study.
	Teacher training	Teacher training was not reported for this study, but teacher resources are available at the Saxon website, including telephone and email access to customer service and educational representatives (in each state).

a See symbol key on page 7.

SOURCE: Reproduced with permission from the U.S. Department of Education.

McEwan and McEwan (2003), in their book *Making Sense of Research*, offer a model that can guide the challenging tasks associated with using research. The McEwan model offers an eight-step series of questions to help guide educators with understanding the research they are using:

- Read the research, and ask the right questions.
- Ask the causal question, Does it work?
- Ask the process question, How does it work?
- Ask the cost question, Is it worthwhile?
- Ask the usability question, Will it work for me?

- If the answers are satisfactory, consider implementation in your own classroom, school, or district.
- Finally, ask the evaluation question, Is it working for me?
- If the answers are satisfactory, continue implementation. If not, solve the problems or drop the program.

McEwan's process is fundamentally sound for building organizational capacity. The first step to addressing the deficiencies in your classroom, school, or district is to identify the areas that are not in compliance with your state requirements that can result in sanctions under NCLB. For example, suppose you have data that indicate a large percentage of students throughout your school district are not meeting state proficiency standards in mathematics. The data indicate the problem is most significant in grades 5 through 8. First, do a literature review of available research using the McEwan questioning process. Then, review the information that is available on the What Works Clearinghouse site on middle school mathematics programs. Finally, review instructional strategies in a small learning community. A collaborative school improvement team working on these three activities will gain the knowledge that will ultimately enable it to implement a successful intervention.

Shawn Arevalo McCollough, principal of Gainesville Elementary School in Georgia, identified 125 pupils who were a grade or two behind in reading and math. McCollough undertook reform activities in his school that led to significant success in student achievement, particularly with his non-white and poor students. One of those activities was administering tests every 9 weeks to the students that measured their knowledge of various components of Georgia's statewide curriculum. The staff analyzed the results and prepared future lessons to address the areas that were deficient (Freedman, 2004). Although many might debate McCollough's use of tests and his focus on the deficiencies, his work with the staff helped them acquire the necessary knowledge to ensure students were learning what the standards required in Georgia. That process will ultimately enable his school to be successful in its quest to comply with NCLB.

Summary

This chapter discussed knowledge acquisition. In addition, I suggested organizing data retreats using teams; there is no argument that they have an equal and important role in knowledge implementation.

Instead of relying on information and programs that lack credible evidence that they work, educators who want to use federal dollars must look to research or evidence or both that support their decisions for program recommendations under NCLB. Although it is fair to acknowledge there is considerable conflicting debate regarding conclusions about what works, the more sophisticated practitioners become as consumers of scientifically based research, the better able they will be to make such decisions.

Gathering data, using it properly, and supporting corrective actions with credible research- and evidence-based programs will lead to successful school improvement initiatives. Using credible and relevant data can eliminate intuition or guesses about implementing new programs. Data will also provide concrete evidence regarding progress toward meeting specific goals.

There is an abundance of resources to acquire research-based knowledge. I am not suggesting that you rely on the U.S. Department of Education as your only resource. There are many education researchers, think tanks, regional education laboratories, universities, professional organizations, and others that can provide credible information to guide school improvement work. The WWC is reliable and will provide a positive first step toward helping educators find credible research information. This book is not written to tell you what resources to use but, rather, to help you determine if those resources pass a reasonable standard of acceptance and will help students achieve more academic success in your schools.

Once you have acquired all the information, the next task is to manage it. In this information society, people are often overwhelmed by the amount of information available. Consider what happens when you use a simple Google search on the Internet.

Interestingly, Google was created to manage information. Some of that information is not credible, however, so it is important to be aware of how to distinguish between what to use and what to eliminate. With so much data available, it must be made user-friendly to teachers and administrators to help them make informed decisions. In Chapter 4, I discuss knowledge management using data warehouse software.

Marilyn Krajenta, principal of a school in Round Lake, Illinois, that was nominated for a No Child Left Behind Blue Ribbon Award from the U.S. Department of Education, summarizes the quest for the challenging school improvement required by NCLB. Principal Krajenta explains that the key to improvement in her school was a renewed focus on reading and a redoubled effort by teachers to ensure that students are progressing with state standards in mind. She states that many of these things are really research-proven practices: "We're putting into practice those things that are effective and letting go of those things that are not"(as quoted in King, 2005).

Action Ideas for Knowledge Acquisition

Remember, school improvement teams should not rely only on the What Works Clearinghouse. There are a number of professional education organizations, informative Web sites, and leading educators who can provide informed guidance on program development and instructional strategies. The key task for school officials is to ask the right questions regarding the success of these resources in school improvement and to carefully check their references. In conjunction with the WWC, the federal regional education laboratories are trusted sources of information on research and development. The laboratories provide a considerable number of reference materials that support their work, and they are often distributed free. Each regional education laboratory (there are 10) is under contract to the U.S. Department of Education through the IES. The laboratories have been serving their regions for many years and have established working relationships with their constituents. It is important to review the laboratory Web site to determine if their work supports your specific school improvement initiative.

Other Research Organizations of Note

The American Educational Research Association (AERA) (www .aera.net) is a professional organization dedicated to improving education by promoting dissemination and practical application of research results. It is an international organization and offers a substantial number of research reports. Using AERA as a research resource for school improvement work will connect practitioners with researchers and their work.

CRESST is the National Center for Research on Evaluation, Standards, and Student Testing (www.cse.ucla.edu). The CRESST Web site includes reports, newsletters, policy briefs, a parents' page, and a teachers' page. In addition, there is an overheads link that includes presentations made by their staff throughout the year. The site allows access to previous years and provides considerable research information.

For a variety of information, particularly on science and mathematics, The National Academies (www.nationalacademies.org) is an excellent resource. Once you access the site, also go to the National Research Council page for additional education information.

The Wisconsin Center for Education Research (www.wcer.wisc .edu) provides research on a variety of education topics:

- Teaching, learning, and professional development
- Educational policy and accountability
- Student learning and achievement in mathematics and science
- English and writing instruction
- Child care, family, and community programs
- Higher education
- Assessment and intervention in special education
- Educational technology

The Wisconsin site also provides links to other research sites.

MDRC (www.mdrc.org) is an organization committed to learning what works to improve the well-being of low-income families. The Web site includes an education section that contains information on school reform, after school programs, and adult learning.

For information on testing, Education Testing Service (www .ets.org) is a useful resource. There are a number of research reports available, including some on characteristics of minority students who excel on the SAT as well as on dropout rates and standards-based reform.

Although not a particularly old organization, The Education Trust (www2.edtrust.org) has earned a respected reputation for its work to support education reform that works in both K–12 and higher education.

One of the largest and oldest research organizations is the American Institutes for Research (www.air.org), which performs behavioral and social science research. Some of its education work includes student testing and assessment, school reform, school finance, and education technology.

The RAND Corporation (www.rand.org) publishes informative research studies. The RAND research supports a variety of education topics.

For evidence-based information on professional development, the National Staff Development Council (NSDC) (www.nsdc.org) has a comprehensive Web site. In addition, the annual meeting of NSDC offers an incredibly large number of presentations in a variety of strands. It is a meeting that is aligned to the specific needs of the attendees. School improvement teams should carefully review the professional development standards of NSDC as the basis for their school or district professional development programs.

Finally, consult the Council of Chief State School Officers (www.ccsso.org) and the Education Commission of the States (www.ecs.org) because their work is highly informative and offers considerable knowledge about policy and implementation of school reforms.

4

Knowledge
Management

In an era of information overload, it is important to know how you will manage knowledge so that it is both readily accessible and usable (Figure 4.1). Too much information can be overwhelming, but, contrarily, failure to use relevant information when it is appropriate can have a devastating effect on successfully implementing school improvement plans, which are critical to No Child Left Behind Act (NCLB) work.

My reviews found what I think is a very practical definition of knowledge management. Amrit Tiwana (2000) says it is management of organizational knowledge for creating business value and generating a competitive advantage. Tiwana notes that knowledge management "enables the creation, communication, and application of knowledge of all kinds to achieve business goals" (p. 5).

As the sanctions of NCLB become more severe each year and ultimately require school improvement plans, it will be very important to consider and act on the information that identifies the reasons a school has not been successful. Thus, Tiwana's (2000) definition of knowledge management for business can be applicable for educators who, under NCLB, must create, communicate, and

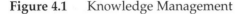

Figure 4.1   Knowledge Management

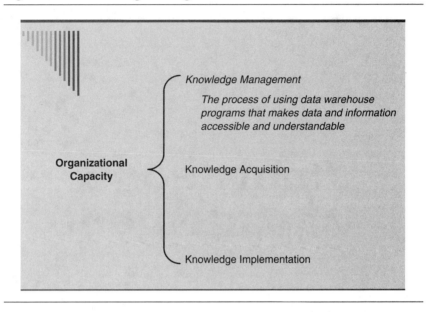

apply knowledge in ways that will enable them to meet specific achievement goals, teacher quality requirements, and improve school programs that are not effective.

Finding and knowing what the data indicate about student achievement and the instructional practices that need to be improved will be essential tasks for educators. Thinking that professional wisdom is a better alternative may only lead to further problems if that wisdom is intuitive and not based on evidence of practices and programs that have been demonstrated to work. Even the most experienced professionals should rely on what data and research can tell them.

In a national best-seller about baseball, Michael Lewis (2003) states the following about data:

> To the extent you can eliminate both [beliefs and biases] and replace them with data, you gain a clear advantage. Many people think they are smarter than others in the stock market and that the market itself has no intrinsic

intelligence—as if it's inert. Many people also think they are smarter than others in baseball and that the game on the field is simply what they think it is through their set of images/beliefs. Actual data from the market means more than individual perception/belief. The same is true for baseball. (p. 91)

Lewis's thoughts about data are applicable to education. The more we know about what is working and what is not working, the more likely appropriate interventions can be used that will be successful. Although it may not be prudent in education to ignore beliefs and biases, data clearly tell a much more accurate story.

Another interesting baseball anecdote about data is one more reminder about the potential danger of relying on intuition. Consider the plight of Grady Little: Little's failure to use the knowledge (data) that was obvious and readily available to him ended up costing him his job. The situation arose during an important game between the historic rivals Boston Red Sox and New York Yankees in an American League Championship Series. Grady Little was the manager of the Red Sox, and his team was leading the Yankees by a score of 5 to 2 in the seventh and final game of the series. The pitcher was Pedro Martinez, the best pitcher on his staff. When New York began to rally, Little relied on his intuition and left Martinez in the game despite knowing the data he had was clear that once Martinez had thrown more than 100 pitches his success and ability to get hitters out were significantly diminished. The Yankees began hitting Martinez's pitches and went on to win the game (Schwarz, 2004, p. ix).

Grady Little did what many educators have a tendency to do—rely on what they intuitively think will work rather than use programs and strategies that are supported by research and evidence demonstrating they work. NCLB was written in a way that requires using data and evidence- or research-based programs. Knowing how well all students are demonstrating an understanding of specific learning standards is critical information. Having that information readily available and making timely decisions regarding intervention strategies for students needing additional assistance can make the difference between their success and failure in the core subjects.

Under NCLB, schools are required to transform their work to a culture of using data and research to support their school improvement work. Transforming this work in an organization is not an easy process. John Kotter and Dan Cohen, both acclaimed change researchers, state that transforming means the adoption of new technologies, major strategic shifts, process engineering, mergers and acquisitions, restructurings into different sorts of business units, and attempts to significantly improve innovation and cultural change (Kotter & Cohen, 2002). Although not all of Kotter and Cohen's concepts directly apply to educators, clearly, adoption of new technologies, major strategic shifts, thinking about restructuring to meet accountability goals, and attempts to significantly improve innovation and cultural change are key concepts that school leaders must consider. It will be a critical knowledge management task to successfully implement an NCLB culture in schools of standards-based curricula, to be able to present assessments to determine if those standards are met, to manage the data addressing the needs of specific subgroups of students, and to maintain information on the highly qualified teacher requirements for all the teachers.

These accountability challenges are different from those of the past. The pressure is on school leaders to assure policymakers that achievement gaps are narrowing between all students, including those with limited English proficiency or learning disabilities and those of different ethnicities and gender, and that teachers are highly qualified with proper credentials. Under NCLB, schools can suffer serious consequences for not meeting these requirements.

It is more important than ever to manage knowledge in schools—that knowledge is primarily data encompassing staff and student demographic information, student achievement results, and research. The research knowledge requires a systematic cataloging of the information that can be used throughout the school district to support the highest priority school improvement initiatives.

Knowledge management sounds simple, but one need only spend time in a school to discover the overwhelming amount of information thrust upon teachers and administrators to understand how challenging their work can be. An excellent example of why knowledge management is important can be demonstrated by considering Google, the highly popular Internet search engine. Google is a relatively young company, yet it has a significant influence on how people acquire and manage knowledge using the Internet. The creation of Google began as a school project to determine how to make information easier to find on the Internet. These researchers, who became the creators of Google, realized what many educators frequently experienced as they too were inundated with a bewildering, disorganized list of every Web site that contained words for which they were searching (*60 Minutes*, 2005). Too much information makes it difficult to focus on what is really important. The need for an "education Google" might help overburdened teachers and administrators with the incredible amount of brochures, reports, updates, and newsletters piling up on their desks.

This chapter offers a foundation for knowledge management from the classroom to the school and to the district that supports the fundamental underpinnings of NCLB. This does not mean that it is just an NCLB model but, instead, it is also a commonsense process to develop an accountable instructional management system. It is founded on the belief that there needs to be student demographic information and achievement data that can be used by classroom teachers and building and district administrators to inform their work at the different school organizational levels. Teachers need to use formative assessments and technological programs that help them teach with standards-based curricula and monitor student progress. Teachers and administrators need to use their state assessment programs to inform their school improvement planning based on the proficiency scores of their students. Teachers and administrators must use other relevant assessment data, such as nationally normed testing, to guide their work. The most important aspect of this process is to manage this information in a manner that makes it accessible, relevant, and understandable.

To be successful with NCLB, compliance will necessitate a new and different perspective on the role and importance of teachers to the education system. True accountability will stem from the classroom, where it will be essential to ensure that every student meets state proficiency standards. Also, when students are not meeting these standards, teachers will be expected to recommend intervention strategies to help these students. Educators are hearing more about applying the "medical model" to their work. The analogy here is that the classroom teacher is the general practitioner, and students with significant learning problems may need to be referred to specialists who understand how to modify and deliver instruction in different settings and styles, similar to how the medical profession uses specialists such as neurologists, surgeons, and ophthalmologists. What must be avoided is the tendency to overly diagnose those students who do not truly need a specialist. It is far too costly to refer them to a specialist when the problems can be corrected in the regular classroom by teachers who have the training and appropriate working conditions to meet those needs.

There are technology programs to help make these tasks of monitoring student achievement easier and more meaningful. One program, offered by the Northwest Evaluation Association (NWEA), is an example of what can be used to help classroom teachers with formative assessment. Using the NWEA program during the school year provides teachers ongoing monitoring of student achievement progress on learning standards. The superintendent of public instruction in the state of Washington announced a Web-based electronic learning plan system to help educators plan, monitor, manage, and evaluate student achievement. Another program, SchoolNet, can reduce time and cost for managing student learning profiles. SchoolNet is a data warehousing software package that can integrate school data and help educators with decision making—the data transcends the classroom, school, and district. These programs are examples of how knowledge management can be applied in an education setting.

NWEA, SchoolNet, and the Electronic Individual Learning Plan are not the only programs that can be used for managing knowledge, but they are examples of the concept of knowledge management and how to make it readily accessible and useful for practitioners working on school improvement. These programs empower teachers to make decisions based on relevant data regarding student achievement. Without a focus on teachers and empowering them with the knowledge and skills that are evidence based, there is little chance any school will make adequate yearly progress (AYP) or target the subgroups in NCLB that lead to the reduction of serious achievement gaps.

Understanding Formative Assessment

The types of data that schools will need to successfully implement NCLB follow a path from the classroom to the building to the district. It begins in the classroom, however, and the knowledge a teacher gains about each student is important to plan intervention strategies for those students who are not meeting proficiency on the expected learning standards. This information is often found in the state assessments and norm-referenced testing administered by schools. Unfortunately, this information is often not used by teachers because it is not in a format or managed in a way that enables them to access it easily or align it to their classroom lessons. There is a body of research, however, that supports using formative assessment, an ongoing process of assessing student progress as they move through the curriculum.

Formative assessment was analyzed in a study conducted by the Assessment Group of the British Educational Research Association (Black & Wiliam, 1998). The basis for the research was that in terms of systems engineering, education policy treated the classroom as a black box. The study was founded on the idea of using formative assessment—self-assessment done by teachers and their students to adapt their work on an ongoing basis. A compelling case was made that ongoing classroom assessment of student achievement toward reaching state standard proficiency goals would provide teachers with essential information for appropriate intervention strategies. The following were primary questions used in the study:

- Is there evidence that improving formative assessment raises standards?
- Is there evidence that there is room for improvement?
- Is there evidence about how to improve formative assessment?

The implications of this study are not just for NCLB requirements but also for an improved system of learning for students that starts with the classroom. In general, the findings from the researchers' work were as follows:

- Innovations that include improving formative assessment practices produce substantive learning gains.
- Improved formative assessment helped low-achieving students more than others. (This finding would have significant implications for working with the subgroups of NCLB because any strategies that result in higher achievement could lead to meeting AYP.)
- Information about pupil performance received by teachers is insufficiently used to inform their work. (In this instance, the basic requirements of NCLB actually begin in the classroom, particularly with state standards at each grade level in reading and mathematics and how well students are learning them. A formative assessment plan that periodically produces information regarding student achievement on the specified learning standards would lead to better intervention strategies.)
- Feedback to any pupil should be about the particular qualities of their work with advice on how to improve.
- Tests and homework exercises were found to be an invaluable guide to learning, but they must be clear and relevant to learning goals.

There were other findings contained within the study, but the important point is that knowledge management, particularly at the classroom level, is key to implementing the fundamental learning principles of NCLB. A number of colleagues I worked with in England often referred me to the Inside the Black Box study. A subsequent study, titled *Working Inside the Black Box* (Black, Harrison, Lee, Marshall, & Wiliam, 1998), expanded their findings. Interestingly, the reports of both studies were contained in two very small booklets that made a compelling case for clear learning standards, ongoing assessment in the classroom to determine whether students are becoming proficient with those standards, and using the knowledge from those assessments to inform teaching and learning strategies—all critically important tasks for NCLB work.

Formative assessment took on greater significance when the Education Testing Service (ETS) introduced an online item bank that teachers can use to produce classroom assessment aligned with state academic content standards (Olson, 2005). The ETS Formative Assessment Item Bank enables teachers to create classroom tests and quizzes to track student performance throughout the year. Using the formative assessment will enable teachers to modify instruction and use interventions that will help students be more successful on state proficiency tests. The ETS product clearly supports the findings from the Inside the Black Box study and can be used to inform instructional practices that may lead to improved student success under NCLB.

Examples of Knowledge Management Products

Although I use some commercial products as examples of how they can be used for knowledge management and NCLB school improvement initiatives, I cannot overemphasize the fact that there are a number of other similar products available. I am not endorsing these products but have spoken with educators who have used them and have heard their positive feedback about them. School officials need to set the criteria for their knowledge management products and interview the vendors to determine whether the products meet their specific needs.

Measures of Academic Progress

The Northwest Evaluation Association (NWEA) uses Measures of Academic Progress (MAP), a data-based management tool for assessment, to accurately provide knowledge regarding a student's academic progress and growth over time. More impressively, NWEA's software enables teachers to get immediate feedback, an important task for planning intervention strategies.

Although some acknowledge that school leadership and great teaching are arts more than sciences, the ability to use data to measure what really works with students is an indispensable asset. NWEA's MAP system removes grade-level barriers and measures individual student growth in specific subjects. NWEA results provide specific and immediate information about the strengths and weaknesses of individual students. When used with DesCartes, NWEA's learning continuum, teachers have access to specific learning objectives for each student or group of students in their classrooms. On a district level, administrators search for specific patterns within demographic subgroups as they plan effective, meaningful, and rigorous instruction that is individualized for all students.

According to NWEA officials, initial reactions to using these data included comments such as "More testing will take more classroom time" and "I'm not sure what to do with this data," but reactions such as these were short-lived. After training and involving teacher leaders and building principals, most everyone becomes enthusiastic about the possibilities of what can be done. They learn how to use data to inform instructional practices.

Today, all teachers use simple charts to show their students what they accomplished the year before, how they are growing during the current school year, and what they need to accomplish during the next school year. In addition, they use the data to show each individual student and his or her parents the student's learning progress.

Assessment data drive all NWEA's improvement processes, such as quarterly management reviews. Once each academic quarter, teachers and principals gather multiple measures of achievement data to show trends in goal areas over time by subject, teacher, student, ethnicity, and so on. Then they review student and teacher interventions, attendance data, and strategies to address low areas.

Building principals provide curriculum directors with analysis of the data and their plans for intervention. NWEA data are also used to plan professional development for teachers and staff and inform administrators about what specialists may be needed.

As a result of the data-driven culture, educators who have used NWEA have witnessed cumulatively increasing achievement scores and are in line to meet federal and state mandates for demonstrating AYP. Most important, districts can now analyze how each of their initiatives has resulted in student growth. Having quantifiable data eliminates guesswork or hunches and helps to pinpoint what resources will best help to ensure that every child learns, grows, and thrives (Figures 4.2 and 4.3).

Electronic Individual Learning Plan

The Electronic Individual Learning Plan (EILP) is a product that is being used in the state of Washington to help school districts improve student learning and track achievement progress. An important feature of EILP is that it allows schools to more easily create personalized student learning plans for all students. EILP responds to the need for teachers to address learning needs of students other than those identified with disabilities but still struggling with academic achievement. Under NCLB, teachers using this type of technology to individualize their instruction will be more effective in meeting the diverse needs of their students and ultimately helping them make consistent progress.

EILP essentially helps teachers with six important instructional tasks:

Figure 4.2   NWEA student progress report

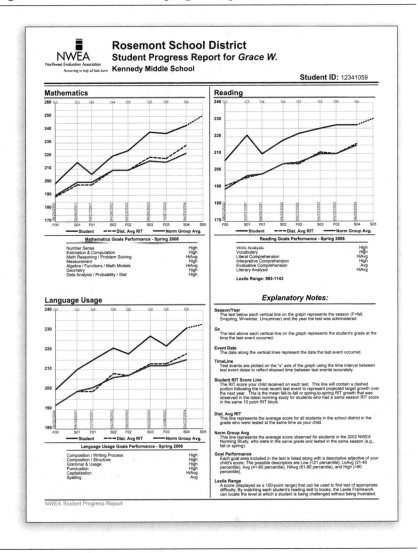

SOURCE: Reproduced with permission from the Northwest Evaluation Association.

- Identify students not meeting academic standards.
- Analyze student performance data to identify student needs and to group students when appropriate.
- Identify potentially effective interventions to assist students in meeting academic standards.

Figure 4.3   NWEA class breakdown report

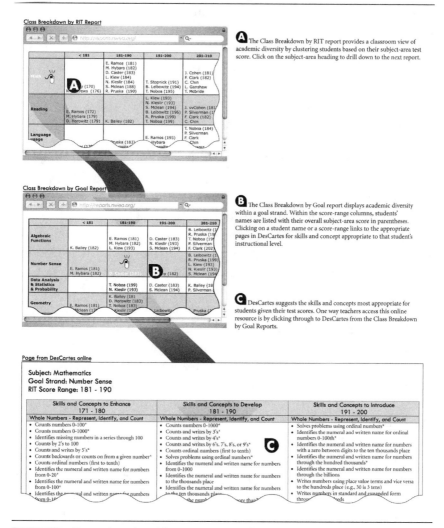

SOURCE: Reproduced with permission from the Northwest Evaluation Association.

- Match identified student needs with appropriate interventions both individually and as a group.
- Communicate the plans to the participants (i.e., parents, teachers, specialists, administrators, and students).
- Implement and monitor the plans to determine their effectiveness and identify needed modifications.

The software facilitates these tasks by identifying students directly from state assessment data, allowing grouping of students by performance level on state assessments, providing a database of potential interventions, and recording the groupings and assigned interventions. In other states and in other settings, these tasks are accomplished through more time-consuming management processes, including the use of Word processed files. EILP is automated and far more conducive to monitoring school improvement work.

Karen Farley, a consultant with the Puget Sound educational service district, stated that using EILP will reduce the amount of time needed to assemble a student's test record and generate an individualized plan from 45 minutes, costing thousands of dollars in staff time, to 15 minutes (Trotter, 2005).

EILP helps teachers plan, monitor, manage, and evaluate their students' achievement by identifying specific needs and applying research-based interventions. Because of the general nature of the state of Washington's large-scale testing, these results do not adequately diagnose an individual student's problem. For example, students who are struggling with reading are identified by the state assessment. Instead, targeted reading diagnostic assessments can be used for students struggling with the reading requirements of the state test. These diagnostics, the results of which are recorded directly into IELP software, can be used to group students for interventions where appropriate. This saves both time and effort compared to creating a specific individualized intervention for each student while still addressing individual needs. Once students are appropriately grouped, suitable interventions can be identified and implemented to address specific student needs in the more efficient group setting. As students advance in the skills on state performance standards, ongoing assessments, also embedded in the software, can be used to predict the students' likelihood of success on future administrations of the statewide test.

Those charged with school improvement acknowledge the high cost in staff time for truly individualized instruction. EILP software provides two advantages. First, EILP offers targeted instructional interventions that guide teacher decision making

Figure 4.4 Student Learning Plan

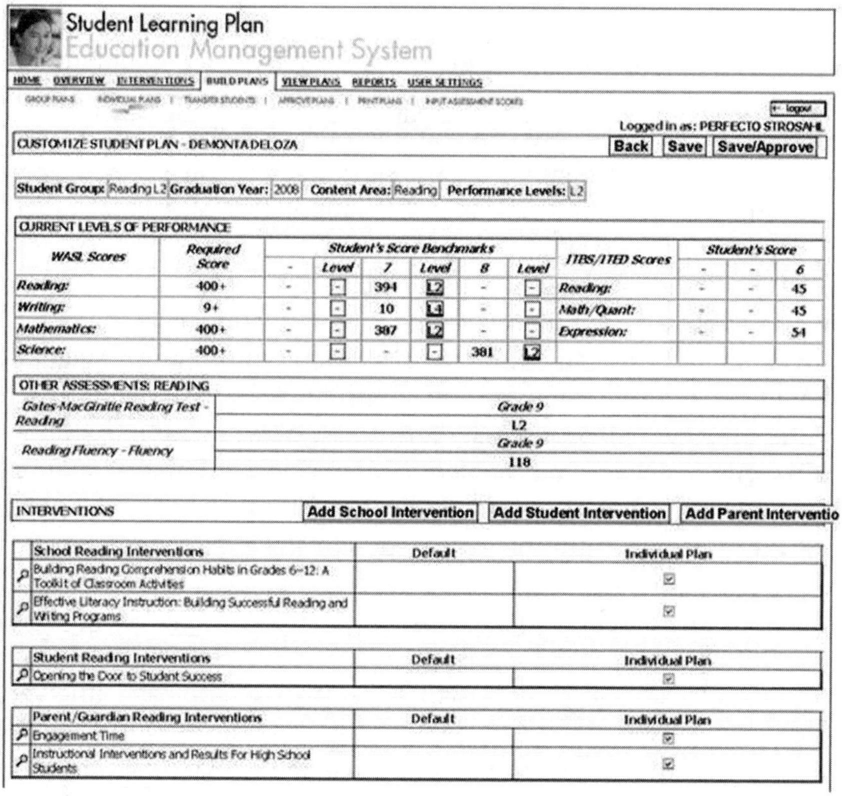

around creating personalized plans, enhancing teacher under-standing, and providing experience with research-based strategies. Second, the ability to strategically assign different groups of students different interventions, with individual students belong-ing to multiple groups in unique combinations, allows plans that are individualized at the student level but managed at the group level (Figure 4.4). This avoids a scenario of intensive and costly cre-ation of learning plans one student at a time. Together, these two advantages can help teachers maximize the efficient engagement of students who are in need of special instructional interventions.

Instructional Management Solutions

For school districts to effectively increase student achievement while complying with the requirements of NCLB, it is imperative that they implement instructional management solutions (IMS). These systems generally serve as the hub of district instructional activity, incorporating data warehousing, decision support, curriculum management, instructional planning, professional development management, and assessment. Districts need access to a variety of student data and instructional information as well as a means to collect new data. These data include much of the operational data historically housed in student information systems, including student demographics, enrollment, attendance, discipline, and special programs. Additional data, including student achievement results, teacher education/certification information, state learning standards, and curriculum and instructional materials, are also generally incorporated into the IMS. These systems also provide access to credible research and programs to support school improvement planning efforts. SchoolNet is a comprehensive IMS that fulfills these needs.

As an IMS, SchoolNet provides the means to manage, analyze, and act on essential student performance data through the lens of NCLB. Data-driven decision making is a high-stakes responsibility for district officials under NCLB. Districts that use data well and make improvements based on that knowledge have a significantly greater chance of successfully complying with the daunting challenges of NCLB than those that do not.

In the age of NCLB, data management is a critical infrastructure component for school districts. SchoolNet offers an instructional data mart, a student-focused data warehouse that provides a repository to store current and historical student data (demographics, attendance, enrollments, withdrawals, discipline, special programs, standardized tests, benchmark tests, course grades, etc.). The instructional data mart serves as the foundation for all reporting and analysis available throughout the SchoolNet IMS (Figure 4.5).[1] The IMS enables a wide variety of district users to analyze data,

Figure 4.5 Assessment results by ethnicity

Pre-Formatted Reports: Demographic Overview

⊙ Tools: ▢ Save Report ◈ Create PDF File ⋙ Batch Create PDF Files

Data Selections
↪ Show Selections ✎ Edit Data Selections

School: KENNEDY ELEM ⌄ Previous View • Next View

Count of Students by Grade Level

K	1	2	3	4	5	6	7	8		Total Unique
45	43	47	60	61	54	60	56	60		475

Percentage of Students by Gender

	K	1	2	3	4	5	6	7	8	Total Unique
Male	51.1%	34.9%	44.7%	53.3%	42.6%	48.1%	60.0%	53.6%	53.3%	234
Female	48.9%	65.1%	55.3%	46.7%	57.4%	51.9%	40.0%	46.4%	46.7%	241

Percentage of Students by Ethnicity

	K	1	2	3	4	5	6	7	8	Total Unique
American Indian	2.2%	0.0%	0.0%	0.0%	0.0%	0.0%	0.0%	0.0%	0.0%	1
Asian Pacific	0.0%	0.0%	4.3%	1.7%	3.3%	0.0%	0.0%	3.6%	1.7%	8
African American	4.4%	2.3%	6.4%	6.7%	14.8%	5.6%	1.7%	3.6%	10.0%	31
Latino	8.9%	4.7%	10.6%	8.3%	1.6%	11.1%	8.3%	10.7%	8.3%	38
White	77.8%	93.0%	78.7%	83.3%	78.7%	83.3%	90.0%	82.1%	80.0%	393
Other	6.7%	0.0%	0.0%	0.0%	1.6%	0.0%	0.0%	0.0%	0.0%	4

SOURCE: Reproduced with permission from SchoolNet.

assess performance, and individualize instruction—all toward the goal of increasing academic achievement.

The SchoolNet IMS is composed of a series of modular, Web-based applications. The SchoolNet IMS serves as the district's sole instructional portal, allowing the district to store all its instructional content and information in one place. Serving as a portal, the SchoolNet IMS provides the ability for districts to integrate software packages from third-party vendors through a synch program.

The reporting and analysis application, "Account," generates the reports district users need to analyze school and district performance through the lens of NCLB. The Account module enables you to track student performance and predict progress toward AYP goals. You can also generate student and school growth reports, analyze standardized and benchmark test results, track trends in disciplinary incidents and student mobility (transfers, withdrawals, and graduations), and review district demographic trends.

A useful feature of Account is the series of AYP Stoplight Reports. These reports can be configured for schools or student subgroups, and they use an intuitive color-coding system to indicate AYP status. Green stoplights are used for groups that are meeting AYP, yellow for groups that are meeting AYP by only a slim margin and therefore designated an "area of concern," and red for those groups not meeting it. The AYP stoplight reports enable users to obtain valuable information, including data on individual schools, demographic subgroups, and specific student results. Making this information instructive and readily available to those who need it is essential for managing school improvement (Figures 4.6 and 4.7).

The "Assess" application enables districts to effectively prepare and administer formative assessments to test student comprehension of essential learning objectives (Figure 4.8). It also provides information to target teacher intervention by allowing users to create and schedule districtwide benchmark tests. To support the creation of the tests, Assess enables users to create and bank new test questions, select from multiple existing test questions contained in the Assess item bank, or import assessment items developed by third-party publishing companies. From a knowledge management context, users can develop districtwide testing calendars and track the progress of data collection at the district, school, and individual student level.

The "Align" application is the curriculum management and instructional planning application (Figure 4.9). With this module, you can create multiple districtwide or school-based curricula, align those curricula with district and state standards, organize scope and sequence, and set pacing guides for courses throughout

Figure 4.6   District AYP stoplight

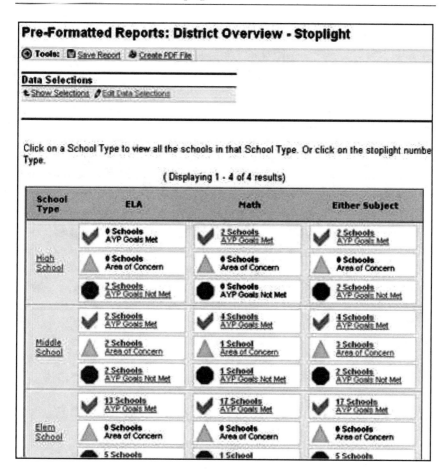

SOURCE: Reproduced with permission from SchoolNet.

the district. Align also enables districts to organize standardized instructional units, lesson plans, and teaching resources into a centralized materials bank that allows for consistency in the delivery of standards-based instruction. In addition to the curriculum and instructional resources in Align, users also have access to student performance data. When using Align, teachers can differentiate students in their classes based on comprehension of key skills and learning objectives to develop valuable customized individual

Figure 4.7   School subgroup stoplight

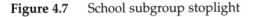

NCLB Category	ELA	Math
Summary	● AYP Goals Not Met	✔ AYP Goals Met
Male	● 222 Students Not Proficient	✔ AYP Goals Met
Female	✔ AYP Goals Met	✔ AYP Goals Met
Ethnicity: African American	▲ Area of Concern	✔ AYP Goals Met
Ethnicity: Latino	▲ Area of Concern	✔ AYP Goals Met
Ethnicity: White	✔ AYP Goals Met	✔ AYP Goals Met
Ethnicity: Other/Multicultural	△ Area of Concern Insufficient Data	✔ AYP Goals Met Insufficient Data
Ethnicity: Asian	✔ AYP Goals Met Insufficient Data	◍ Area of Concern Insufficient Data
Ethnicity: Native American	✔ AYP Goals Met Insufficient Data	✔ AYP Goals Met Insufficient Data

SOURCE: Reproduced with permission from SchoolNet.

learning plans. The power of technology can make knowledge management readily available to all in much the same way the Internet has brought information to its users in new and functional ways.

Finally, the "Outreach" application is the communication and collaboration module that enables districts to create a venue for the

Figure 4.8   Assess home page

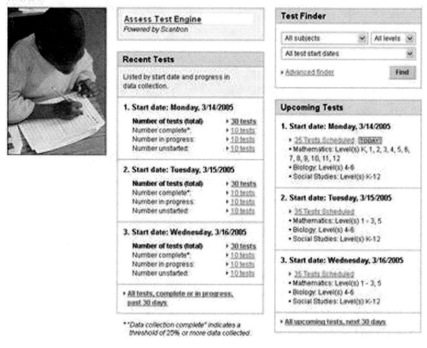

SOURCE: Reproduced with permission from SchoolNet.

disclosure of public information for NCLB compliance as well as a full range of day-to-day news, announcements, and class materials (Figure 4.10). Outreach provides a K- through 12-specific content management system for the creation of district, school, and teacher Web sites as well as shared calendars, discussion forums, and a districtwide directory.

A useful feature of the Outreach module is "Family Access," which provides parents and guardians online access to important information about their children, including course enrollment, academic record, special program enrollment, teacher notes, individualized learning plans, and standardized test results.

Figure 4.9   Curriculum alignment

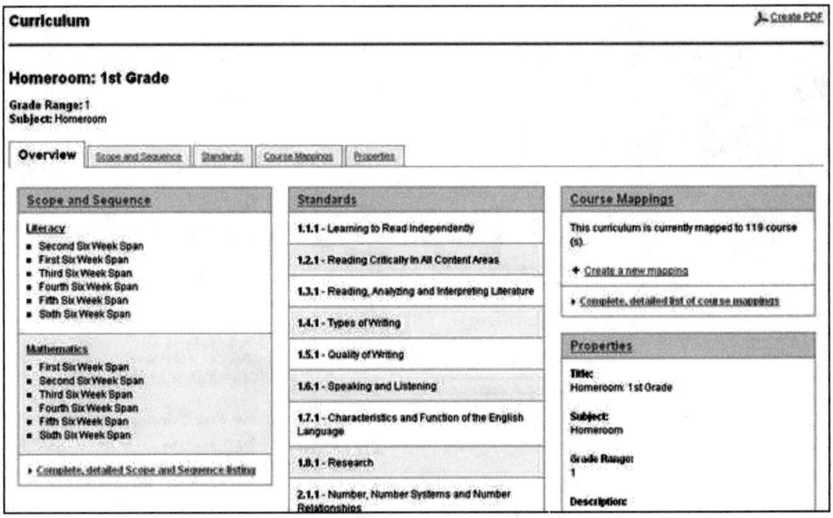

SOURCE: Reproduced with permission from SchoolNet.

Summary

The knowledge model for building organizational capacity, knowledge acquisition, knowledge management, and knowledge implementation is not composed of separate and discrete tasks. Rather, it is a continuous and simultaneous process that focuses on providing knowledge in schools and enabling them to be accountable for their students' learning success. Knowledge management, the task of creating, communicating, and applying knowledge, emanates from the use of data to inform school improvement work. For Grady Little, not using known data resulted in a serious mistake and in a serious sanction: He lost his job as manager of the Boston Red Sox. Little's situation is a sports metaphor that can be applied to education. NCLB is a law that requires the culture of schools to be evidence and data based in their decision making to avoid the consequences of sanctions.

Figure 4.10 Outreach

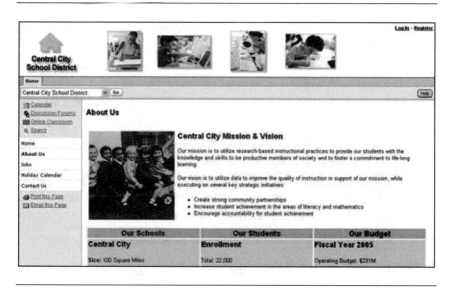

SOURCE: Reproduced with permission from SchoolNet.

Schools must be accountable for the quality of their teaching staffs by meeting certain certification and subject knowledge requirements and for the achievement of all students. Although not a perfect law, the use of what has been learned by practitioners during the first years of NCLB implementation is resulting in some modifications to it. Understandably, these modifications will be slow and likely based on evidence demonstrating that certain aspects of the law are not working as intended. Without managing the knowledge and using it to inform NCLB work, however, the intended goals of improvement are unlikely to be attained.

An Action Idea

Lane Mills (2005, p. 8), an assistant superintendent, wrote a useful article on how to choose a vendor for data management software.

Mills provides the following suggestions:

- Be sure the solution is flexible enough to meet current and anticipated system needs.
- Ask the vendor for information about its successful experiences with data management that are aligned with your needs. In addition, get references so you can check on the vendor's claims.
- Obtain a detailed cost for ownership of the product, and ask about infrastructure requirements.
- Ask about the costs for training and ongoing support.
- Ask about system security and system maintenance costs and also where the equipment needs to be set up and any special provisions for cooling and so on.

Mill's suggestions are useful steps when reviewing what type of data management system you plan to use.

Note

1. All school data in figures are fictitious.

5

Knowledge Implementation

To build organizational capacity with the knowledge model requires knowledge acquisition using data and research. Those data and research must inform school improvement initiatives to comply with the requirements of No Child Left Behind (NCLB). Using technology such as data warehouse software programs, the process of knowledge management can be undertaken. Making the data and research easily accessible and presenting them in a structured context are important if you expect teachers to use them. These components for building organizational capacity are critical to making informed decisions, but unless they are used with consistency throughout the organization, the knowledge-gathering work will not be of much use. Once you have acquired and managed the knowledge, it is time to implement it throughout the organization (Figure 5.1). That is done through high-quality professional development.

This book is a conceptual effort to keep the process of building organizational capacity uncomplicated and focused. It places emphasis on the idea that possessing knowledge is what will lead to the type of success called for in education accountability laws

Figure 5.1   Knowledge Implementation

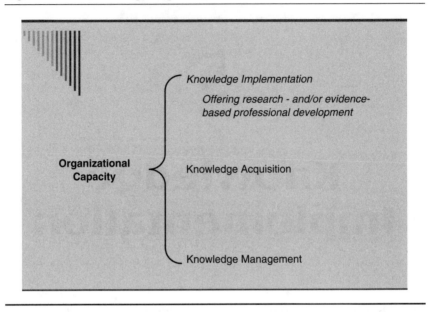

such as NCLB. Sometimes, adherence to basic fundamentals to build organizational capacity is all that is required. There is already more than enough for educators to do. It is time to retreat to basic routines that apply to their work. The notion that using specific data to better understand problems that identify key school improvement issues and finding credible research to resolve those issues is likely to lead to successful improvement initiatives.

In school improvement, educators often work to reinvent the wheel when all that may be needed are adjustments that improve on what they have been doing. The process for program improvement should be similar to the evolution of a successful product that has improved over time. For example, consider television. We have entered a new era of television viewing with concepts such as digital, plasma, and high definition. To some, however, it is still only a box with a picture—albeit a much better picture that has evolved through continuous improvements. Educators need to build on what they already know and continue to learn how to solve many of the basic problems NCLB was written to address. There is already a substantial body of knowledge about teaching and learning that can be used to support your work.

Effective leadership for knowledge implementation necessitates articulating a coherent vision for the planning and implementation of professional development with a laser-like strategy. It also requires new thinking about school administrative hierarchies and who best to lead these initiatives. It is not just the traditional administrators who can undertake these responsibilities. The more contemporary thinking regarding the use of teams that are led by teachers is more in line with how professional development will be transformed into quality learning opportunities for teachers in the future.

Knowledge implementation using research- or evidence-based professional development or both will ensure that there are highly trained and informed employees in the organization. The ability of educators to make knowledgeable and informed decisions is just as important as it is for airline pilots or doctors when they find themselves in challenging situations in which normal procedures are not working and effective modifications to a work plan are necessary.

According to Anthony Alvarado (2005), the former leader of the New York and San Diego school systems, professional development has to be focused on putting the knowledge into practice immediately and not just on knowing what good teaching is or reading about strategies that work. Knowledge and practice are not the same things, he notes, and strategies can fade when not put into practice immediately.

Alvarado's comments make a strong case for the knowledge model to build organizational capacity. He also issues a compelling challenge to support my thoughts regarding the use of the knowledge model as an integrated, ongoing process. You need to begin with knowledge acquisition, gathering the data and research, and then put that knowledge into an accessible delivery process. Once the process has begun, however, it is not static. Instead, it is ongoing and requires due diligence—a periodic process of carefully reviewing the information pertaining to the issue. To move that knowledge into the organization's daily operations requires knowledge implementation—a well-structured, research-based, and relevant professional development plan that continuously incorporates current thinking on improving the quality of teaching and student achievement.

Imagine having a painful knee problem. You see a knee specialist, who informs you that you need surgery. During the consultation, you learn that the doctor attends professional development programs for a few hours once per year and programs planned by medical associations 2 or 3 days per year. You also discover that these programs are unrelated to the doctor's core responsibilities—to be up to date on the latest knee surgery techniques—but rather focus on medical ethics, better patient scheduling practices, and forming medical partnerships. None of the medical association programs are intended to improve the doctor's medical expertise about knee surgery. As the patient, you are placing your faith in a physician who is not up to date with the latest information on the most current surgical techniques. This lack of knowledge may result in a longer convalescing period and potentially harmful longer-term effects from the surgery—all because the doctor's professional development programs were unrelated to the core strategies needed to improve his surgical techniques.

Although it is not possible to generalize about all school districts in the United States, enough is known to support a premise that, for the most part, the scenario about the knee doctor is not unlike what many teachers go through year after year. How many teachers have gone to work the first day of the school year and spent the entire day listening to irrelevant speeches that had little to do with their work or the mission of their school district? How many of those teachers attend professional development days throughout the year that include offerings that have little relevance to their teaching assignments? NCLB requires professional development programs funded with federal dollars to be research based, and enough credible evidence exists that the activities should be of a reform type, sustained over time, relevant to the participant's work, collaborative, benchmarked, aligned to the district and school missions, and structured to improve student achievement and teaching strategies. Anything less in this NCLB environment is wasting valuable dollars and teachers' and administrators' time.

Professional development is a critical component for building organizational capacity. There is no substitute for a well-trained workforce. Teachers need to be provided sufficient opportunities to collaborate with their peers regarding their work. They need to be made aware of contemporary theories of education supported by evidence and research demonstrating that they are effective. Also, they must be able to implement these strategies into their daily work. Professional development is the vehicle that enables them to accomplish this task. It should be no different for teachers than it is for athletes who practice their skills on a daily basis to improve. Athletic practices are typically ongoing, benchmarked, and aligned to what the players need to do to be more successful. They are carefully planned by coaches who regularly evaluate what they need to do for their teams as a whole to be successful. The concept is not complicated: Identify what needs improvement, and work diligently on the techniques that will lead to it.

According to Richard Elmore (2005), a noted school improvement researcher, schools do not suddenly get better and meet their performance targets. He states,

> Improvement is a process, not an event. Schools build capacity by generating internal accountability—greater achievement and coherence on expectations for teachers and students—and then by working their way through problems of instructional practice at ever-increasing levels of complexity and demand. Right now no infrastructure exists to provide continuous support for failing schools. (p. 27)

Elmore's comments are an important caution regarding how important it is to create the right infrastructure to enable failing schools to succeed.

Jack Welch (2005), the former CEO of General Electric and a successful author of business books, says that a job should "feel somewhat challenging going in and make you think you can do most of the work, but there are certainly skills and knowledge the job requires that you don't have yet" (p. 260). He goes on to say that "employees should feel that they are going to learn something" (p. 261). Welch's philosophy is that employees need to continuously learn how to improve their work, and to do this requires sufficient time for them to participate in those learning experiences.

In a paper written for The Finance Project on preparing and training professionals (Neville, Rachel, Sherman, & Carol, 2005), education was compared to six other fields, with the following conclusions:

- Most of the comparison fields had developed more uniform standards for entry into the field, preparation program approval, and in-service training.
- Education was the only profession that allowed individuals to practice before completing their defined licensure program.
- Clinical experiences and induction in education were less structured and less consistently supervised than those in other fields.
- Education was the only field that required managers to have separate licensure.

These findings support what many educators have said for years. They should be considered a rationale for seriously reforming how teachers are prepared and trained for their work. Clearly, the transformation of professional development for teachers will require substantial consideration of finding time for the activities and, at the very least, reconsidering how funds are currently being used for training and compensation. It may also mean increasing the funds for teacher professional development.

Professional development is often one of the first items to be cut from a budget when finances are tight. The logic of that decision is often perplexing given the critical need for teachers to be knowledgeable about their content and using effective instructional strategies. Professional development planning is just one of the important tasks for successful schools. There are others, and it is important to incorporate them as well into a strategic plan for the district.

In our book, *Achieving World-Class Schools* (Kimmelman & Kroeze, 2002), the metaphor of genetics is used to identify a process for comprehensive strategic planning to achieve world-class schools. We noted that just as human beings are complex, living, dynamic organisms involving the interaction of systems, organizations are similar in their operation. Chromosomes, genes, and DNA are the basic foundations for the manifestation of human beings, and in successful organizations the critical core structures are developed by leaders applying their fundamental principles using evidence or research or both to support them. It is also noted that, as a metaphor for planning, chromosomes are core structures, genes are fundamental principles, and DNA is the research or evidence to support the fundamental principles. It is no less a conceptually comprehensive process in organizations than it is in biology.

We suggested that there were six core structures essential to organizing a world-class school system. They are divided into two basic categories: capacity building and teaching/learning. Included in the capacity-building category is professional development that is research based and founded on a set of fundamental principles that support improved teaching and learning. No school district can be successful without recognizing the importance of ongoing training for its staff. Using the metaphor of genetics makes what seems complex much simpler.

Resource A of this book is a case study on professional development from the John Edward Porter Professional Development Center at Learning Point Associates. This case study offers an example of how difficult and time-consuming professional development planning and implementation can be for a school improvement planning team. The case study also demonstrates that when a staff is committed to improving its work, it can be done despite challenges, and the need for high-quality staff training is essential if improvement is the goal. This case study should serve both as a guide and as a lesson for knowledge implementation in a school.

Finally, an excellent professional education organization that advocates for high-quality professional development is the National Staff Development Council (NSDC). NSDC offers a substantial amount of information on professional development or professional learning, a term that its executive director, Dennis Sparks, uses. Sparks has long been an advocate for high-quality professional development in schools, and his suggestion of changing the term to professional learning is certainly applicable to the ideas contained in the knowledge model.

NSDC also provides standards for professional development. The standards offer guidance on context, process, and content. Using the NSDC Web site (www.nsdc.org) would be invaluable when applying the concept of knowledge implementation to school improvement planning.

Knowledge Implementation Using Professional Development

Resource A also provides an authentic case study of a comprehensive professional development planning and implementation process in a school district. This section is intended to provide an overview of some professional development research, activities, and thinking on the topic. There is scant scientifically based research available, but those who work in schools can intuitively describe the essential activities needed to improve their professional learning opportunities. One does not need to invest large sums of scarce resources to understand that to improve the knowledge of workers, their experiences have to be of high quality and sustained over time to reinforce their new learning. They also have to be collaborative, actively engage the participants with their colleagues, and use data and research that are relevant and aligned to their work.

Despite the paucity of research on professional development, a study on whether it changes teaching practice was completed for the U.S. Department of Education in 2000, with the following conclusions:

- Professional development focused on specific higher-order teaching strategies increases teachers' use of those strategies in the classroom. The effect is even stronger when the professional development activity is of the reform type (i.e., teacher networks or study groups) rather than traditional workshops or conferences. It was also noted that it is important to provide opportunities for active learning; that the agenda must be aligned with the teacher's goals; and that the activity involves teachers who teach the same subject or grade or who teach in the same school.
- Teachers experience professional development that varies in quality from one year to the next, and those teachers in the same school can have very different professional development experiences.
- There was little change in overall teaching practice from 1996 to 1999, but some teachers individually demonstrated a moderate variation in their classroom practices.

This study supports a radical departure from the type of traditional professional development teachers have been receiving because it suggests that conferences and onetime workshops will not result in much improvement. Thus, it is incumbent on school leaders to begin a transformation of professional development planning—one that incorporates collaborative working opportunities for teachers; sustains the activities over an extended period of time; aligns them with their goals; and uses delivery strategies that are more contemporary, such as topical DVDs, online courses, and study groups.

Rasmussen, Hopkins, and Fitzpatrick (2004) use another baseball metaphor for describing good professional development. They say that good professional development is like "a perfect curve ball—it's all in the commitment, planning, effort, and practice" (p. 16). They identify the key components of professional development as being coherent, research based, and capacity building. In other words, coherent professional development is aligned with school improvement efforts and agreed upon goals. Research based means that all decisions are based on careful examination of effective practices. Capacity building means the participants agree to work together to learn new skills to become more self-sufficient. Rasmussen et al. cite six steps for successful professional development planning:

- Gather and analyze the data.
- Set student learning goals, and align school improvement efforts with those goals.
- Define instructional strategies that address learning goals.
- Identify what staff need to know and be able to do to in order to implement new strategies.
- Define professional development initiatives, and develop an action plan.
- Create a professional development evaluation plan.

Their writing on professional development is consistent with the basic requirements of building organizational capacity using a knowledge model. The professional development work must be considered a high priority for teachers. Although there are many who might debate the importance of investing in high-quality professional development for teachers, the country of Finland represents a good example of why teachers are so important for successful schools. In an article that discusses why Finland's schools may be the best in the world, Pekka Himanen, a renowned scholar who earned a PhD at age 20, states that the high quality of Finnish education depends on the high quality of Finnish teachers (Kaiser, 2005). Himanen supports the notion that investing in building the knowledge base of the teachers leads to improved performance. A well-planned professional development program can achieve that goal. Also, his comments support the need to offer teachers high-quality professional development.

Study Groups

McLaughlin and Talbert (as cited in Steiner, 2004, p. 4) found in their study of 900 educators that teachers who belonged to professional communities were better able to adapt to the challenges of teaching today's students. The concept of professional development groups was also supported by Newmann's (as cited in Steiner, 2004, p. 4) research, which found that more successful schools' professional development planners used a combination of local and external expertise.

There are a multitude of available professional development grouping or learning community concepts. It is important that these decisions be made by the participants. Empowering the participants to make decisions regarding their professional development will not only lead to better planning of the activities but also enhance their commitment to the program. For a comprehensive professional development resource, consider using *Powerful Designs*, published by the National Staff Development Council (Easton, 2004).

Lesson Study

A popular collaborative professional development activity being used more frequently in the United States is the result of work done by James Hiebert and James Stigler (1999) during their research on the Third International Mathematics and Science Study video study (nces.ed.gov). Hiebert and Stigler discuss in detail the practice of lesson study used in Japan to refine individual lessons (p. 111). Japanese teachers jointly develop, teach, and refine single lessons over time to ensure they are taught effectively. Although lesson study is a cultural practice in Japan, a number of U.S. teachers have undertaken the process, adapting it to their specific circumstances. The authors note that if you want to improve teaching, the most effective place to do so is in the context of a classroom lesson.

Teachers are the essential ingredient for improving schools and student achievement. Professional development activities such as lesson study fulfill the need to bring teachers out of the isolated environment of teaching and offer collaborative working opportunities for them to improve instruction. Bringing teachers together without facilitation and providing relevant data and research to support their school improvement work will not only waste time but also not lead to improvement.

Other Professional Development Activities

Tom Guskey (2000, p. 22), one of the leading education writers on professional development, says the major models of professional development are

- training;
- observation/assessment;
- involvement in a development/improvement process;
- study groups;
- inquiry/action research;
- individually guided activities; and
- mentoring.

Guskey's suggested models offer some conceptual activities for knowledge implementation. He defines training as a process involving a presenter or team of presenters who share their expertise with the participants. Training formats include group presentations, workshops, and simulations. In observation, teachers observe each other and offer feedback. Observation of a taught lesson is an important part of lesson study, mentioned previously.

The development/improvement process is closely aligned to knowledge building. In development work, teachers are involved in writing curriculum and course standards or designing new programs or both. The collaborative work is an important component of professional development. In development work, it is often worthwhile to use external consultants who are recognized for their expertise and success in their work. The expertise of the consultants gives substance to what the teams need to accomplish.

According to Guskey (2000), study groups bring focus and coherence to improvement efforts, especially if groups are carefully structured, well trained, and well supervised. The concept of learning communities is receiving much attention in education journals.

One caveat, however, is that to spend a great deal of time on learning how to organize them seems far less important than doing the substantive work that is required of them. School improvement planners need to place a higher priority on involving teachers in substantive content and teaching strategy sessions than on devoting time to discussing how to organize the learning communities.

Action Research

Research on what is happening in a specific environment can be informative; it is equally important, however, to be aware that most action research is only applicable to the group being studied, and the findings are not readily transferable to other settings. The potential topics for action research are unlimited. Some examples of action research that teachers may want to do are analyzing student achievement on a particular unit they are teaching, whether various strategies being used in the classroom improve discipline, or how using incentives might increase homework completion. The action research can be helpful when trying to better understand a local school initiative.

Glanz (1998, p. 24) identifies the key steps in action research:

- Select a focus.

  Know what you want to investigate.

  Develop some questions about what you want to learn.

  Establish a plan to answer the questions.

- Collect data.

  Surveys

  Interviews

  Portfolios

- Analyze and interpret data.

- Take action.

  Decide what to do based on what you learned.

Individually Guided Activities

Another of Guskey's (2000) models for professional development is individually guided activities. These activities span a wide range from enrolling in a content-based graduate education program to developing a growth plan aligned to specific goals to improve teaching strategies, content knowledge, and student achievement, or all three. It is important to ensure that the activities are focused on specific goals. Often, teachers take courses or participate in professional development that have little or no connection to improving their work. If the motivation for participating is merely to gain credit for movement on the salary schedule, it is likely that the activity may not be overly rigorous.

Finally, Guskey (2000) mentions mentoring; currently, no other model is receiving more attention. What is particularly striking about the new impetus to offer mentoring programs as part of professional development is that it should be considered a normal part of the orientation process for new teachers. Also, professional development should not only incorporate mentoring but also be followed with ongoing induction planning.

Teacher Leaders

School administrators are encouraged to consider the concept of teacher leaders for professional development activities. This leadership should be real leadership, however. It should actually empower the teachers to accomplish the goals of the activity in much the same way that principals and other line administrators are delegated responsibilities.

According to Crowther, Kaagan, Ferguson, and Hann (2002), teacher leadership "facilitates principled action to achieve whole-school success. It applies the distinctive power of teaching to shape meaning for children, youth, and adults. And it contributes to long-term, enhanced quality of community life" (p. 10). The authors found in their research on teacher leaders that the leaders have certain characteristics in common:

- Teacher leaders convey conviction about a better world.
- Teacher leaders strive for authenticity.
- Teacher leaders facilitate communities of learning.
- Teacher leaders confront barriers.
- Teacher leaders translate ideas into action.
- Teacher leaders nurture a culture of success.

Teacher leadership responsibilities should not be offered without the necessary support and training. No teacher should be asked to lead a group without some understanding of the basic responsibilities of leadership. The teacher must be able to facilitate a group and recognize that not all participants are always cooperative and that dealing with difficult people can be part of the leadership challenge.

The teacher leader should be aware of the parameters for the group's work. Also, it is not fair for administrators to assign a project to a teacher-led group and then not only reject but also never use the group's work if it conformed to the parameters set for it. More important, it will make it more difficult in the future to get people to do the work if they have not found the experience to be fruitful.

Teacher leaders should also be knowledgeable about their work. They should have expertise that is respected by the participants and district administration. A more detailed presentation on teacher leadership, provided by the U.S. Department of Education Teacher-to-Teacher program, can be found at www.paec.org. The presentation includes a video, PowerPoint, and other materials. (In some states, using this link can count for credit toward meeting the state's High, Objective, Uniform State Standard of Evaluation requirements to be "highly qualified.")

Lessons for Districtwide Reform Leadership

After reviewing the many options for school improvement work, consideration should be given to what Fullan, Bertani, and Quinn (2004) state are the key lessons for understanding how districts implement large-scale change. The authors cite 10 key components for leaders to implement to build school capacity and improve student learning:

- A compelling conceptualization—teams of people creating and driving a clear, coherent strategy.
- Collective moral purpose—everyone in the organization has a responsibility to change the larger education context for the better.
- The right bus—the right structure for getting the job done.
- Capacity building—essential for everyone in the organization and important to develop new leaders.
- Lateral capacity building—connecting schools in a district.
- Ongoing learning—continually refining the strategy.
- Productive conflict—disagreements occur during change and need to be handled productively.
- Demanding culture—high pressure, high support.
- External partners—business groups, foundations, and community-based organizations.
- Focused financial investments—putting money into projects that pay off.

Summary

It should be apparent that once knowledge is acquired and managed, it needs to be used when implementing school improvement strategies. That does not mean accepting claims from vendors or consultants who proclaim that their products and processes have led to incredible growth in student achievement. Credible research and evidence are derived from sources that are external to those making the claims. So, if a textbook publisher states that its reading series has led to remarkable student achievement gains and the publisher commissioned the research, the claim is likely tainted. That is why there is a need for the What Works Clearinghouse, and it is hoped that it will be an independent and unbiased source for educators to turn to when planning their school improvement work.

The focus on teaching using the professional development models for knowledge implementation is a critical planning task. All the models should incorporate the concept of knowledge acquisition by providing the participants data and research to support their learning activities. In the planning, the following questions should be asked and answered: What are the objectives for the project? What data have been collected, and how are they being used? and What research is available to support the strategies being considered to make the intended improvements? In addition, all information must be readily accessible to those who need it.

NCLB includes provisions that require teachers to be highly qualified. The provisions stipulate that teachers in the core subjects must have

- a bachelor's degree;
- full state certification as defined by the state; and
- demonstrated competency, as defined by the state, in each core academic subject he or she teaches.

There has been considerable debate regarding the highly qualified teacher requirements, but there is also ample evidence indicating how important it is for teachers to be knowledgeable about the subjects they teach. For the most part, the research has focused on mathematics and science, and it has been supported by comparing teachers who have a college major in their teaching field to those teaching a subject out of their specialty field or with less academic background.

Dr. Grover J. Whitehurst, director of the Institute of Education Sciences, made the following statement in a 2002 speech at the White House Conference on Preparing Tomorrow's Teachers:

The effects of teacher training on academic achievement become clearer when the focus becomes subject matter knowledge as opposed to certification per se. The research is generally consistent in indicating that high school math and science teachers with a major in their field of instruction have higher achieving students than teachers who are teaching out-of-field. . . . These effects become stronger in advanced math and science courses in which the teacher's content knowledge is presumably more critical.

Regardless of the debate over certification and licensure, it makes sense to plan professional development programs for teachers that are content based and organized to help them learn more about the subjects they teach. We need to ensure that teachers are well prepared for their assignments, and that they are career-long learners continually expanding their knowledge about content and teaching strategies.

Virginia Richardson (2003, pp. 401–406) wrote about the dilemmas of professional development and her concern about the lack of research evidence used in planning programs. Richardson said that, based on many studies, several characteristics for professional development should be included in the plan. It should

- be schoolwide;
- be long term with follow-up;
- encourage collegiality;
- foster agreement among participants on goals and vision;
- have a supportive administration;
- have access to adequate funds for materials, outside speakers, and substitute teachers;
- develop buy-in among participants;
- acknowledge participants' beliefs and practices; and
- make use of an outside facilitator/staff developer.

School improvement programs should build that research base into their knowledge acquisition, management, and implementation organizational capacity model. We now live in a global knowledge society, and many business leaders and policymakers are speaking publicly about their concern that the United States may be in danger of no longer being a world leader in the knowledge industry. Think about what countries are developing many of the technologically smart products you purchase and, more important, where they are designed. It would not be fair to imply that K–12 education should shoulder the entire burden of resolving the global economic competition issue for the United States. It is fair to conclude that the education profession has been slow or reluctant or both to undergo serious transformational change to meet the needs of a contemporary society. The concepts of online education, effective use of technology for learning, and even conceptually different types of schools, such as charter schools, are only a small part of the continual change coming in education. The most effective way to address these changes is to ensure that the professionals involved in education are well trained and are held accountable for successful work.

Action Idea From Dr. Ken Arndt

Dr. Ken Arndt, superintendent of School District 300 in Carpentersville, Illinois, was asked to write his thoughts regarding the use of data and school improvement from the leadership perspective of a superintendent. The following are Dr. Arndt's thoughts and suggestions on how superintendents should consider new concepts of leadership in the NCLB era:

> My emphasis regarding the need for data and research to be easily accessible to educators should be the same priority for superintendents when working with school boards, community leaders, and local media. Superintendents sometimes forget that in order for organizational capacity to be implemented, all stakeholders, especially elected board of education members, need to be brought along in the process just as much as parents, teachers, and administrators. Superintendents cannot perform this task alone.
>
> Whether superintendents are willing to admit to this reality, society demands increased accountability with data-driven results. The days when a superintendent's

recommendations are not challenged are long gone. Superintendents must have quick and accurate data in order to prove their statements. The data administrators use to make decisions must be accessible to the public. Many times, administrators have been publicly embarrassed and/or chastised when the data does not support their statements. With the widespread use and access of the Internet, accurate statements are a critical component in developing administrators' credibility with their board, staff, and public. The general public no longer wants to hear that results might not be known until a decade later.

It has been my experience that when school districts contract services from a respected outside agency, it helps lend credibility to the process from a board member's perspective. But, superintendents must be actively involved in the decision-making process and demand accountability from the outside contractors.

Just like most superintendents are involved in a multi-million dollar construction project, or the employment of key staff members, they also need to be involved in shaping the education plan for their students. It should be the responsibility of the superintendent to frequently report back to the school board, community leaders, and media the results and accomplishments of their school improvement initiatives. A superintendent's active presence and voice will contribute toward building the capacity for organizational change.

Long-term, sustained professional development is critical to the success of the teaching staff. Professional development cannot become a one-day-per-year event that meets a state-imposed mandate. In Community Unit School District 300 in Carpentersville, Illinois, approximately 35% of the teaching staff has 5 years or less teaching experience. In collaboration with the local teachers' union, the board of education wanted to see a mentoring program organized that would offer new teachers the opportunity to develop the skills necessary to effectively perform their duties. We were not interested in one or two beginning-of-the-school-year training programs, but instead wanted an extensive 2-year process that would incorporate best teaching practices utilized by experienced mentor teachers.

The mentoring process is data and research driven. Partnerships for assistance and external review were established with a local university and we acquired funding for 3 years to implement the program. The process has proven to be very effective and was recently named as one of the most outstanding teacher mentoring programs in the nation by the National Education Association and Saturn Corporation.

Professional development is a critical component for developing organizational capacity. There is no substitute for a well-trained workforce. Sometimes, administrators and board members need to be reminded of this simple, but most fundamental, aspect of an effective organizational development responsibility. By partnering with outside agencies and using your own workforce, highly effective results can take place.

Our experience, however, in dealing with effective school reform initiatives using outside agencies has been mixed. Some school reform contractors have been guilty of making claims that cannot be proven or their promises kept. It is disappointing to a staff to be prepared for a facilitator only to learn hours before he or she arrives that the presentation had to be canceled. If, and when, such situations should occur, complaints should not only resonate from the teaching staff but also from the central office and superintendent. As the adage goes, the squeaky wheel gets the most attention, so should be the case when professional development programs fail.

School reform is certainly not inexpensive. And, contrary to the claims of some professional development providers, no one program will cure all school challenges.

Superintendents who value professional development should work extensively with their boards of education and staff to make certain the resources are available for high-quality programs. And, they should work toward developing the internal capacity to implement change. Administrators should look closely at the existing human resources available before collaborating with an outside agency. One should be leery of professional development that is based on fancy three-ring binders. Likewise, superintendents should be leery of professional development providers who reside hundreds of miles away from their districts and who do not have a sufficient workforce to be in the district as scheduled.

Superintendents need to realistically and critically review their own capacity for organizational change. Small districts that might have one or two staff members assigned to teach a curriculum will certainly have greater difficulty implementing best practices based on research than buildings where a dozen staff members may be employed in that specific curriculum. If this is the case, consider collaborating with neighboring school districts, universities, or regional education centers.

My claim that teachers need to have basic group facilitation skills for change to be effective cannot be emphasized enough. Administrators should not assume that every teacher can effectively lead other teachers toward organizational change if the administrator, himself or herself, is not willing to provide the needed assistance for them to be successful. Just like one would never assume inexperienced drivers could operate an automobile, effective group facilitation skills are essential for groups to work well and accomplish their goals.

The No Child Left Behind Act mandates that districts employ only highly qualified teachers. Who can fault that? I have never met any administrator who does not want to hire a fully qualified teacher. However, the teaching field is very competitive today, and one should not assume that there is a multitude of highly qualified teachers in hard-to-fill teaching areas such as bilingual education, special education, foreign languages, and advanced mathematics and science.

At the beginning of the 2005–2006 school year, Community Unit School District 300 had 11 teaching positions that remained vacant in difficult-to-fill teaching areas despite an intensive and aggressive recruiting campaign. One of those vacancies, bilingual behavioral disabilities, had been vacant for 2 years. The district has only been able to fill this position through long-term substitute teachers, which according to NCLB does not meet the requirement of a highly qualified teacher.

Here, I present a very straightforward perspective on the importance of professional development in school improvement programs and provide a perspective and a goal that every school district should achieve. It has been my experience that most school districts are not reluctant to change, but the political, social, and economic constraints districts work under present their own unique set of circumstances. But challenges can be overcome if the chief school administrator of a district, the superintendent of schools, establishes himself or herself as an educational leader and not just an educational manager.

6

Courageous School Leadership and the Challenge of NCLB

Creating a Challenge Mind-Set Using Stories

It will not be easy for many schools to successfully meet the requirements of No Child Left Behind (NCLB). Nor will it be easy to apply the knowledge model to build organizational capacity for those schools. Creating a knowledge organization will require time, commitment, passion, effective leadership, ability, credible data, research, resources, and, most certainly, the funds to support it. Yet there is no other alternative for the schools that are struggling to meet the NCLB requirements but to work diligently to get better and improve the results of their students' achievement. If they do not, they face the possibility of being reconstituted under the sanctions of NCLB. Daunting challenges can be frustrating and, worse, create mind-sets that encourage giving up.

Politics notwithstanding, it is interesting to note that one of the criteria President George W. Bush set for appointing cabinet secretaries in his second term was to choose people with "extraordinary personal stories of having succeeded after overcoming great obstacles" (James, 2004, p. 1). I often use stories about people who overcame significant challenges or obstacles in many of my presentations on NCLB. I have chosen to tell their stories because I think they bring a context to the challenges facing educators with respect to obtaining much higher achievement in their schools and classrooms when attempting to comply with NCLB. Dealing with the NCLB challenge can be similar to the story about the person who was in the hospital for a minor illness and thought it was a horrible experience until he talked to the person in the next room who was battling terminal cancer. There is always a challenge or situation that is more difficult than the one you are confronted with, yet, without a context, it seems as if the situation is insurmountable. Challenges are what can motivate people to achieve higher goals and greatness. The belief that NCLB contains impossible goals tends to discourage some educators from taking them on and simply shrugging them off as impossible.

So why even bother? The changes that are needed to improve education are embedded in the law and provide the basis on which school improvement should be planned. Few debate the ethical and fundamental beliefs regarding what NCLB is intended to do; the real debate concerns the rules and regulations. Those aspects of the law can be changed and, over time, a number of them probably will be. The vision to ensure that truly "no child be left behind," however, is the overriding theme of the law and should remain the mission of every school.

The Broadway musical *Man of La Mancha* includes a highly inspirational song, "To Dream the Impossible Dream." The lyrics tell a story that could be a metaphor for NCLB by describing a quest for a cause because the world will be better for it. For many teachers and administrators, accepting the belief that every student will reach 100% proficiency may just be the "impossible" dream. Yes, NCLB has some accountability requirements that will not be met. Yet making the effort to achieve them is appropriate.

It is important to demonstrate to teachers and administrators, those who are expected to make significant changes to the way they work, that the changes are necessary and can ultimately result in substantial improvement in their work. Surely, NCLB will help many students who might not otherwise have had a serious opportunity to receive a higher-quality education because they are the focus of the law.

The People and Their Stories

Consider some interesting people who overcame significant challenges and obstacles that others thought might be impossible. Their stories highlight the possibilities of success when facing the most daunting challenges. Through commitment, dedication, perseverance, knowledge, and hard work, these individuals often met those challenges with success. The following are examples that provide a better understanding of their mind-sets when confronted with what appeared to be unbeatable odds, yet they succeeded. Ernest Shackleton attempted to cross Antarctica on the ship *Endurance* in the early 1900s (Morrell & Capparell, 2001). The attempt was unsuccessful, but his leadership and the way in which he saved his crew have become a story for leadership classes in universities. Despite horrendous conditions after his ship became icebound, Shackleton led his crew to safety against what appeared to be incredible obstacles without losing any of his men. Shackleton's success can serve as a metaphor for those who may not believe they can achieve the 100% proficiency requirement for all students under NCLB. Although he did not succeed in his original goal of crossing Antarctica, he did fully succeed in what became a more valiant effort—saving the lives of his entire crew after disaster struck. Although some schools may not reach the 100% requirement, substantial improvement on their student achievement may be deemed successful by their states or local communities or both.

In 1999, while on a research sabbatical in Antarctica, Dr. Jerri Neilsen had to treat herself for breast cancer. She not only performed a needle biopsy on her own breast but also administered her own chemotherapy because there was no possibility for her to be evacuated to a hospital. During this time, Neilsen was able to continue to perform her duties for the research project (Neilsen, 2001). Neilsen's work should serve to inspire those who need encouragement to take on challenges that may seem insurmountable.

I often wonder why anyone would want to climb Mt. Everest. Every year, there are stories of how people die trying to scale the summit. People do it, however, simply because it is there to be done. The amazing, death-defying story of how Jon Krakauer (1997) climbed Mt. Everest not only describes the events but also offers the thoughts of someone who endured an incredible journey. As another example, Ruth Anne Kocour, along with a team of nine men, climbed Alaska's Mt. McKinley. Against what seemed insurmountable odds, they survived the worst storm on record to hit Mt. McKinley (Kocour, 1998).

In business, Lou Gerstner of IBM (Gerstner, 2002) and Jack Welch of General Electric (Welch, 2001) transformed their companies and created new organizational cultures to ultimately make them successful again. Their leadership work arguably saved their companies from going out of business. Note that they did not win popularity points with their employees while guiding their companies through these transformations. Sometimes, transformational work has risks. Gerstner's and Welch's experiences, however, may help education leaders better understand the process and consequences of organizational transformation under the accountability provisions of laws such as NCLB. Similarly, public education is being confronted with competition from those who believe parents should have choices about where they send their children to school. To retain the public education system will require risk taking and visionary leaders who are up to the challenges of transforming their schools and making them better.

Finally, there is the story of how Wilbur and Orville Wright ultimately flew the first airplane. The story is incredibly interesting because it is about two common people who had a dream and pursued it. Despite being high school educated and competing against the likes of Samuel Langley from the Smithsonian Museums and other wealthy Europeans who had far more resources, the Wrights succeeded in being the first to fly at Kitty Hawk (Tobin, 2003). They focused on a goal and persevered. Implementing NCLB provisions will necessitate that kind of perseverance by all educators.

In education, Paul Vallas, CEO of the Philadelphia public school system since 2002, has demonstrated that the process of improvement in the most challenging of education situations is possible. He says that what separates effective superintendents from some of the less effective ones is "who has the ability to figure out the financing and who has the ability to create the organizational structure so you can bring these reforms to scale" (www.districtadministration.com). His work, like that of many other unheralded education leaders, is not easy or always politically popular. Under the leadership of Vallas, the Philadelphia School District posted its third consecutive year of growth on state achievement tests. That growth transcends racial and economic demographic groups and is a clear example that even in the most challenging circumstances there is the potential for success (www.philsch.k12.pa.us).

Successful school leaders demonstrate a passion for doing what needs to be done to ensure that their students have an opportunity to succeed in a rapidly changing global society. Moving schools through a transformational process is, as my boss Gina Burkhardt, who has a tendency to always add an extra "really" to emphasize a point, says, "really, really, difficult work."

These examples of successful people and the mental models they offer can provide a context for believing that nothing is impossible. Using their stories as the background for overcoming significant obstacles can present a mind-set for your staff. In his book, *Whoosh*, Tom McGehee (2001) talks about the importance of models and creating a "beginner's mind." These stories get people thinking about overcoming the challenges, not being restricted by them.

A Hopeful Result of Building Organizational Capacity to Implement NCLB

So what might a school that implemented the knowledge model look like in 2013, 1 year before the 100% compliance rule goes into effect? First, we start in 2002 with a fictitious school named McKinley Elementary, led by a dynamic principal who viewed NCLB as an opportunity to try out-of-the-box ideas. He wanted to improve his school's student achievement and offer high-quality professional development to the staff to prepare them for the daunting challenges of NCLB. The following is their hypothetical story.

Let's skip ahead to 2013. McKinley Elementary School is located in an urban area. The school offers classes in grades K–8, and there are 750 students. Fifty percent of the students are Caucasian, 15% Hispanic, 20% African American, 5% Asian, 5% Russian, and the remaining 5% are students from a variety of nationalities. Eight percent of the total student population is identified with disabilities.

There are 42 teachers at McKinley, a principal, and an assistant principal. All the teachers are highly qualified under the guidelines set by their state, meaning that they have a bachelor's degree, full state certification, and have demonstrated subject matter competency in the core content subjects. They participate in an ongoing, sustained professional development program. The goal of the program is to raise student achievement by improving teachers' content knowledge and pedagogy.

During the past 10 years, they built organizational capacity with the staff by following the knowledge model. For knowledge acquisition, they acquired and analyzed data to inform their work. They used their state assessment tests for their local NCLB compliance work, portions of a nationally normed test to benchmark and compare their students' performance on specific content areas to that of their peers nationally, and developed formative assessments to monitor the individual progress of all students in their classrooms.

Teacher leaders direct the professional development program with support from the principal and assistant principal. Much of the professional development work centered on research reports from the Institute of Education Sciences, colleges and universities, and professional organization publications. The teachers worked collaboratively on planning their professional development activities and had the responsibility for operating within an allotted budget.

They also had support from respected external consultants, who assisted them with specialized content knowledge activities in the subjects they taught as well as data analysis from their state and national assessments, writing formative classroom assessments, and pedagogy to inform their activities. The consultants also assisted them with their selection and purchase of knowledge management software. The consultants had no relationship with any of the vendors, and their recommendations were based on the specific needs of the McKinley staff for their knowledge management work.

The teachers participated in regularly scheduled meetings that were designed to replicate the mortality and morbidity conferences used in the medical profession. Doctors participate in these conferences with other doctor colleagues to discuss what went wrong in particular cases or how a better outcome might have been achieved. What is unique about these conferences is that they are private and not subject to public scrutiny. It gives doctors an opportunity to share with their colleagues what are often their most difficult experiences and possible mistakes they may have made while not risking lawsuits (Gawande, 2002). Similarly, McKinley teachers now use these meetings to discuss the problems they are having with their most challenging students. Often, the suggestions made by their peers help them overcome the problems. The teachers enjoy the meetings because they are not supervised by administrators or used in an evaluative process. Their time is used in a constructive manner without a concern that there will be retaliation for not being successful. Instead, they are invigorated through peer support that provides suggestions to overcome the problems they confront in their classrooms on a regular basis.

McKinley teachers are accountable for their work through specific benchmarks and goals they set annually for improved student achievement. The student achievement goals align with their state's adequate yearly progress formula. The teacher leaders meet regularly with the principal and assistant principal to discuss their progress on the goals and what might be needed to support their work.

Interestingly, the culture of the teachers is similar to that of members of sports teams who work together striving for a championship. Just as statistics and goals guide decision making for sports teams' success, the successful accomplishment of the goals from NCLB is determined by using data and setting specific goals. The McKinley teachers' success is determined by achieving their goals as a school faculty, not in individual classrooms or grade levels. Collaboration among the teachers as a team is viewed as essential for them to improve student achievement.

All new teachers are enrolled in the school's mentoring/induction program, which provides ongoing assistance to help them with their teaching responsibilities. Teachers are selected to be mentors by their peers, and only those teachers committed to the program accept the appointment. Selection is based on specific criteria that demonstrate that the mentor teacher has been successful. The program is highly structured and based on research or evidence from mentoring activities known to be effective. The teachers believe the key to their success is that they were empowered to organize and oversee the program and they are held accountable for the results. They sense a high degree of professionalism for their work.

At McKinley, very few teachers seek employment elsewhere. Evaluations of the school by the staff indicate that they enjoy their work environment and the support they receive from their peers and the administration. McKinley's retention rate for its teachers is much higher than that of schools with similar demographics in both the district and the geographic area.

Most of McKinley's students are meeting the state-required adequate yearly progress requirements under NCLB. Although the subgroup of students identified with disabilities is not on schedule to meet the 2013–2014 deadline of 100% proficiency, the school is spared the most severe sanctions as a result of some modifications to NCLB when Congress approved changes and reauthorized the law in 2007. The modifications were minimal but now allow the students with disabilities subgroup to make adequate yearly progress based on continuous improvement and goals set in each student's Individual Education Plan. All other subgroups at the school are meeting the state proficiency requirements.

The public, policymakers, and news media view McKinley Elementary School as a very successful urban elementary school. Those who have studied McKinley attribute its success to the following key factors:

- The emphasis on recruiting highly qualified teachers
- Its research-based professional development program, which focuses on knowledge and provides teachers with the latest information on pedagogy and curriculum content
- The increased staff collaboration, particularly the replication of the medical conferences, which provides a risk-free environment to discuss with their colleagues areas they need to improve or find challenging
- The extensive support from the administration
- The new model of incorporating authentic teacher leadership in the school and the use of data to inform instructional and program decisions

These factors led McKinley's teachers to function as a team, not unlike sports teams led by successful coaches. Coaching is gaining popularity as a helpful practice in business and education. At McKinley, the staff realized that their success could not be defined through individual accomplishments. Rather, their success was based on whether all the students in their school were continuously achieving proficiency. That meant everyone on the staff had to contribute to the overall goal of leaving no child behind.

Whether there will be many McKinley schools in 2014 is speculative. It would be a victory, however, for both Congress and the education profession if the achievement gap is closed and the sanctions schools face under NCLB are reasonable and consistent with practices that will result in the fundamental improvements called for in the law. Certainly, some schools may and should be closed, but it is not politically feasible to assume that all schools will be reconstituted for not meeting every AYP requirement.

7

Final Words

The Knowledge Model

After all this reading about building organizational capacity to comply with No Child Left Behind (NCLB), it comes down to this: Using the knowledge model will enable you to optimize your results for school improvement. NCLB is the most challenging accountability law ever written. The rigid enforcement of it by the U.S. Department of Education has resulted in a great deal of tension between states and the federal government. In the end, many of the disagreements will be resolved. In the meantime, however, there is no reason not to begin working toward schools being more successful by following the logical provisions in the law. To do that means creating a plan that provides for knowledge acquisition, knowledge management, and, finally, knowledge implementation. There is no education cookbook that has all the answers. The knowledge model provides you with a structural framework that will guide you with substantive plans to comply with NCLB.

When I was president of the First in the World Consortium, I was surprised by the number of calls I received from people asking what curriculum we used. They misguidedly believed curriculum alone would result in their ranking with the top achieving nations in the world. As noted previously, some of the schools in the consortium used different mathematics and science curricula and often offered different professional development opportunities for their teachers.

The First in the World Consortium school districts were successful because they followed a proscribed set of criteria for success. They had qualified teachers teaching mathematics and science classes, they had available resources to offer programs that worked for their students in those subjects, and they recognized the importance of providing continuous learning opportunities for their teachers. Yes, the schools were located in higher socioeconomic status communities; although this was a factor, it was not the most important factor that led to their success.

Interestingly, despite the fact that the consortium was successful compared to its international peers, the incredible amount of data and research it generated led to more knowledge acquisition and new school improvement initiatives based on what it learned. Those data and research came from a highly regarded international assessment of student achievement and provided an opportunity for teachers to work with the national Third International Mathematics and Science Study researchers. I do not think there is any better example for local school district educators that could be more substantial for using the knowledge model than what the First in the World Consortium did.

There is too much information available for educators, and my suspicion that NCLB would overload schools with even more data seems to be a reality. It is not about the amount of data that is important, however; it is really about the quality of the data and making them available in useable formats for administrators and teachers. Knowledge management is a daunting process.

Programs such as SchoolNet, Northwest Evaluation Association's Measures of Academic Progress, and the Electronic Individual Learning Plan all support the concept of data accessibility that is useable and understandable. As I noted several times, there are other programs that do the same thing. I mentioned these three programs only as examples. What is most important is that school officials find a quality program and implement it with consistency throughout the organization.

Finally, knowledge implementation is the cornerstone of building organizational capacity. I believe professional development is the key to having a knowledgeable staff. The caveat is that the professional development must be research based and follow the guidelines offered in Chapter 5. Just because a school district offers professional development and invests considerable resources in the activities does not mean it is of high quality. Using poor ingredients to make a meal will not lead to a tasteful experience. Professional development must incorporate research-based information and practices that are known to improve the quality of teaching and learning.

Final Thoughts on NCLB

Most educators are still supportive of NCLB but want it changed to be more realistic with respect to the expectations on student achievement. That will eventually happen. They will not get every change they want, but more thought will be devoted to why some of the subgroups actually will not achieve 100% proficiency. Although there may be some wiggle room on the law, it will not be much. Giving too much leeway would only open the floodgates to changes that would ultimately regress to where federal education law enforcement was prior to NCLB implementation.

As a result of NCLB, there is a new focus on discussing research and using programs with evidence that they work. In addition, far more attention is being paid to the achievement of disadvantaged students, which is certainly a refreshing outcome of NCLB. We all need to be reminded, however, that it is the practitioners who work with students on a daily basis who are making this happen. To many who are critical, however, it is not happening fast enough. We should heed the adage of looking at the glass as being half full instead of half empty.

If you are working diligently on school improvement to comply with NCLB, you should consider inviting your members of

Congress to visit your schools. That visit could result in the members gaining a better understanding of the challenges you are facing under NCLB and may lead to even better education policy in the future.

Finally, do not forget that NCLB is a law that was overwhelmingly approved by a bipartisan Congress. Although President George W. Bush led the process as part of his domestic policy agenda, it could not have happened without the leadership of two key Democrats, Representative George Miller and Senator Edward Kennedy, and two key Republicans, Representative John Boehner and Senator Judd Gregg. When there is an overwhelming bipartisan vote in the U.S. Congress, it sends a clear message that the country supports change. Throughout the country, there are many reform concepts being used in schools. Much more is being said and done with regard to vouchers, charter schools, home schooling, and online education. Although a proposal by President George W. Bush in 2005 to reform high schools did not gain support in Congress, the issue of high school reform has gained momentum with governors of many states and business leaders (see Resource B). To retain the fundamental principles of public schools in the United States will necessitate improving the achievement of all students and ensuring a high-quality teaching force. From my perspective, that can be done by building organizational capacity using the knowledge model.

Resource A

Tibbott Case Study

Building a Team:
Shared Leadership Takes Hold

Soon after its founding in 2001, the John Edward Porter Professional Development Center set out to identify a small number of
pilot sites to receive assistance with designing high-quality professional development. One result was the center's ongoing partnership with John R. Tibbott Elementary School in Bolingbrook,
Illinois. The school's work with the center between 2002 and 2005
highlights how using research-based professional development
can have positive results for student achievement (see Box A.1).

Box A.1   John Edward Porter Professional Development Center

The John Edward Porter Professional Development Center works
collaboratively with school communities to build their capacity to
plan, implement, monitor, evaluate, and sustain professional
development that results in high-quality instruction and increased
student performance. The Porter Center is committed to improving
student learning by helping educators meet state standards and new
federal requirements. Staff help clients use resources more efficiently
and implement proven methods to reach their goals. They have

---

developed research-based, hands-on professional development services that meet each school community's specific needs. The following operating principles guide their efforts in providing the highest quality service to the people in schools who are working to improve student learning:

- Coherent—agreed upon goals
- Research based—all decisions meet a demanding standard in that they are based on careful, systematic examination of effective practice
- Capacity building—working together to learn new skills and understandings with the ultimate goal of self-sufficiency
- Customized—designed according to the unique needs of the client
- Comprehensive—understanding complexity and addressing it effectively
- Cost-effective—producing good results for the amount of dollars invested

Background

John R. Tibbott Elementary School is a K–5 school on the eastern border of a rapidly growing middle-class suburb on the outskirts of Chicago (Table A.1). The Valley View School District currently has 17,000 students, and approximately 1,000 new students enroll each year. Tibbott Elementary is more ethnically diverse than most other schools in the district, with a high concentration of second language learners. Approximately 50% of Tibbott's students qualify for free and reduced-price lunches.

In the 1990s, Tibbott struggled with behavior problems within the school and an often negative reputation within the community. When a new principal was appointed to the school in 1977, he had to deal with a high number of external suspensions and 36 broken windows due to vandalism.

The principal made discipline his first priority. He began by reconfiguring the school improvement team (SIT). He asked a more

Table A.1   Tibbott School Information

John R. Tibbott Elementary School	
Bolingbrook, IL	
Valley View School District	
Community Unit School District #365U	
Grades	K–5
Total enrollment	812
Total district enrollment	15,949
Student characteristics	
Asian/Pacific Islander	5.20%
Black	26.50%
Hispanic	42.90%
White	25.50%
Free/reduced price lunch	53%
Limited English proficiency rate	14.90%
Mobility rate	23.70%
Attendance rate	95.80%
Total instructional staff	54
2000–2001 ISAT performance: Grade 3	
Students meeting or exceeding standards	
Reading	58%
Mathematics	81%
Writing	57%
2003–2004 ISAT performance: Grade 3	
Students meeting or exceeding standards	
Reading	63%
Mathematics	89%
Writing	67%

representative mix of teachers and other staff members to serve and assigned each member of the SIT to lead a cadre of other staff members. Each cadre was made up of approximately six staff members, either grade-level teams or teams of staff members with similar jobs. The goal of this restructuring was to have SIT members disseminate information to the rest of the staff in cadre meetings and to get their feedback as well.

Once the SIT was established and had some experience working together, it introduced some changes in how all staff members implemented two existing behavior management programs, Love and Logic and the Responsible Thinking program. The goal was to have fewer referrals and to build more personal rapport with students. Early success with this effort (the number of suspensions declined and the climate in the school improved noticeably) gained the principal some trust and credibility with the staff. By 2001, student behavior had improved dramatically.

At that point, the principal and the SIT wanted to focus their attention on improving academic achievement, but they were not sure how to proceed. Several veteran teachers had just retired or been transferred to newly built schools, and most new hires had less than 2 years of experience. The No Child Left Behind Act (NCLB) had recently been passed, so there was pressure throughout the district to respond to stringent new accountability requirements. The district had been examining data since the 1970s, but gains were minimal overall. In this climate, the principal wanted to introduce the concept of examining data in a more rigorous way, but he was not able to generate much support for data-driven decision making among the majority of staff members.

In the spring of 2002, the district's new assistant superintendent for educational services attended a workshop at the North Central Regional Education Laboratory (now a part of Learning Point Associates) and met the director of the newly designed Porter Center, Claudette Rasmussen. The assistant superintendent was concerned about academic achievement at Tibbott and had even considered hiring another coordinator on her staff to work exclusively with the school. She invited Rasmussen to visit the district and discuss what services the Porter Center could provide. She was particularly interested in the fact that Porter Center services were aligned with NCLB requirements. After the principal talked to the SIT about the possibility of being a pilot site for the Porter Center, the assistant superintendent met with the Tibbott staff to explain what services they could expect to receive. Because the SIT had been struggling with how to get the staff focused on what they needed to do next to improve student achievement in light of NCLB, it welcomed the opportunity to work with the Porter Center.

Strengths Going Into the Partnership

Tibbott had many strengths going into its partnership with the Porter Center:

- *Respected leadership.* The new principal was well respected and had support within his building. He had a strong assistant principal, who had been an integral part of the improvement process at Tibbott.
- *Strong leadership structure.* There was a strong leadership team in place as well as a system of cadres that allowed the team to disseminate information and get feedback on major decisions.
- *Recent successes.* The school had had a series of successes in the past few years implementing an effective discipline program.
- *Improved morale.* Staff morale was relatively high because of the positive changes in student behavior in the past few years.
- *New staff members supportive.* There were several new staff members hired by the principal who shared his commitment to improving student achievement.
- *Respectful relationship with district leadership.* The district relationship with Tibbott was positive. District leaders were willing to invest resources into improvement at the school but were respectful of the need for the staff to make their own choices when it came to hiring an external provider.

Challenges Going Into the Partnership

Tibbott also had many challenges:

- *Low performance on state tests.* Tibbott was one of the lowest performing schools in the district and the only schoolwide Title I school in the district. In 2002, 57% of the students at Tibbott met or exceeded expectations in all subjects on the state test compared to 64% at the district level.

- *High concentration of English language learners.* Between 1999 and 2002, the percentage of white students at Tibbott had decreased from 45% to 30%, whereas the percentage of Hispanic students increased from 22% to 38%. This sharp increase in a period of a few years put enormous pressure on teachers to adapt their instruction to these second language learners, particularly with the NCLB requirement that all subgroups make adequate yearly progress (AYP) every year.

- *School culture not focused on high student achievement.* Tibbott's staff included many veteran faculty members who had not made significant modifications to their instruction even as the student population became more diverse. Most faculty conversations were about personal interests, not professional concerns. Because of the cadre system, veteran teachers and other staff members had some experience having a say in the school's direction, but many still believed that the principal should make most decisions. They saw it as their job to teach the curriculum. When Illinois Standard Achievement Test (ISAT) scores were presented annually by the principal for third through fifth grades, earlier grade teachers did not pay much attention because they did not believe it concerned them directly.

Key Professional Development Activities and Events—Year 1 (2002–2003)

Data Retreat

The principal was able to bring the SIT to a data retreat in November. At this retreat, they met their Porter Center coach and were introduced to the process of using data to set effective school improvement goals (see Boxes A.2 and A.3). The team was enthusiastic about what they were learning and intrigued by the possibilities of data analysis. They were also pleased to be off school grounds together working on something meaningful. Because this group had been working together for a few years, they felt comfortable with each other.

The principal recalls that the findings from the data retreat were interesting and, in some cases, surprising. The team first collected all the available data—local as well as state-level achievement test scores. They decided to focus on state test scores and break down student achievement by subgroups and by strands, specific skills within subject areas. As part of this process, the team discovered that white students' scores were pulling up the school's average scores dramatically. They also discovered that African American students were doing particularly poorly in some areas. Surprisingly, however, with regard to fifth-grade writing, Hispanic students had the highest scores. The team then developed hypotheses about these findings that they planned to accept or reject after gathering additional data. Several of these hypotheses had to do with external or structural dilemmas, such as staff turnover and student mobility. The overarching hypothesis that the entire team eventually adopted, however, was that they were not focusing enough on specific deficit areas.

At this point, the team had a long discussion about how they would report this information and this process to the entire staff. They concluded that literacy was going to be their initial focus, given the weakness in this area across the board, but they wanted to plan carefully for the next stage. As they conferred, their coach served as a critical friend. She did not offer specific recommendations but asked pointed questions to get them to think further about the issues and decisions they were making. SIT members were very conscious that they were at a critical stage for getting "buy in" from the faculty, and they knew that there would be some resentment about the team's opportunity to attend an off-site workshop. They discussed this and decided to hold a mini data retreat in the spring, during which each SIT member would lead his or her cadre through this same process with their grade-level scores. They also decided to do a further analysis of academic subcategories in reading. They hoped this would empower the staff and allow them to "own" both the data and the hypotheses for themselves.

**Box A.2   Data Retreats: Learning How to Use Information
                to Drive Change**

Real school and district improvement begins when leadership teams
use data to clarify their goals. As teams analyze data patterns for
strengths and weaknesses, they are able to measure the impact of
current strategies and practices on student and staff learning. Ongoing
data study then allows teams to focus on their highest priorities.

The Porter Center's data retreat is a 2-day intensive training in
which district and school teams work together to analyze their data,
develop hypotheses, and, ultimately, leave with meaningful plans for
school improvement. Because in-depth reflective data study is difficult
to do during the busy school year, setting time aside for a data retreat
empowers leadership teams to build a dynamic for focused improvement based on their school's data—on an ongoing basis.

Coaching

The SIT met the Porter Center coach at the data retreat and
immediately warmed to her. They went out in the evening with her
and traded professional and personal stories. They liked her folksy,
down-to-earth style and respected her as a successful former principal who had "walked in their shoes." When she introduced some
team-building exercises that they did not believe they needed, she
modified what she was doing to focus more on the data analysis
process. They felt confident that they could learn from her and that
they could work comfortably with her. From the beginning, she
expressed confidence in them and their ability to make good decisions for students, which was both inspiring and encouraging for
them given the reputation they had struggled with teaching in the
lowest performing school in the district.

The principal and other members of the team also appreciated
the coach's style of coaching. She did not make overt suggestions
as much as push them to consider carefully why they were choos-
ing to go in a certain direction. Her questions focused the group on
the principles of effective professional development. For example,

she stressed that it be continuous and embedded in teachers' daily routine, not a single workshop here or there. She also believed that professional development should be aligned with their highest priorities, and that it should take place over time. Even when the group did turn to her for specific advice, she would respond by saying that they knew their school better than she did.

The coach also had a good sense of humor, which eased some of the tension the group members felt as they made difficult decisions about the direction they were going to take. She pushed them to test their hypotheses about why certain subgroups were not achieving while acknowledging that they had been working with limited information. In general, she approached coaching with the attitude that all teachers want to be successful, but that many times they do not have the information and skills they need. She said, "If they knew better, they would do better."

In addition to the work they did together at the data retreat and the Leadership Institute, the coach spent 4 days on-site supporting SLT as it developed a 3-year professional development plan. During these visits, she would typically sit in on team meetings, and sometimes she would make presentations on topics such as differentiated instruction.

Box A.3   Coaching: Supporting School-Based Leadership

The Porter Center matches a highly skilled coach with each site to work intensively with a site's leadership team, both on-site and online, during the course of services. At the beginning of its relationship with the Porter Center, Tibbott Elementary was assigned a coach for the next 3 years of service. Before working as a coach for the Porter Center, she spent many years in the public school system as a teacher, a human relations specialist for the district, an assistant principal, and a principal (she was District Principal of the Year and the following year was named Principal of the Year for the state). As a coach, she had many of her own experiences to draw from, but she believed her first priorities were to listen, learn, and build trust.

Porter Center coaches visit each school approximately four times a year, spend time in classrooms, present teaching strategies, and sit in on school improvement meetings. The coach's role is to assist a school or district team in the process of developing, implementing, and monitoring staff development in ways that build their organizational capacity to sustain high-quality professional development. Critical roles of the capacity-building coach include facilitating the decision-making process of the team, working with the team to customize plans, helping the team to integrate research-based tools and strategies into their planning, helping the team to select appropriate providers of content-based professional development, and enabling team members to evaluate their plans and assess impact.

The Leadership Institute

The next stage in the process was for the team to return to the Porter Center for a leadership institute in January (see Box A.4). The goal of this institute was to have participants walk away with a solid start on a 3-year professional development plan. Much of the conversation during the institute was about where they wanted to go with their newfound knowledge. What did the research say about effective professional development design? What should their priorities be with regard to literacy? What content and instructional knowledge did teachers need? What were their highest priorities? Their medium priorities? What professional development approaches would have the greatest impact? How could they design professional development activities that were aligned with what they were learning about high-quality research-based professional development? How could they monitor and evaluate whether these activities were having the desired outcomes?

Others who were at this conference, the coach and representatives from the district, observed that this was when the team from Tibbott began to hit their stride and realize what they could do. Since the data retreat, individual members of the team had struggled to redefine themselves as leaders, not mere participants, in the change process at Tibbott. For teachers and other staff members on the team, this meant that they had to be willing to step forward and lead their colleagues. For the principal, it meant sharing real decision-making power with the team. Although this process did not happen overnight, by the time of the leadership institute in January, it was obvious to external observers that progress had been made. One sign of this change was the renaming of the team. They now called themselves the school leadership team (SLT) instead of the school improvement team.

The SLT's highest priorities for the next 3 years, as described in its professional development plan, were to hold the mini-retreat that spring to introduce all staff members to data analysis; to train the entire staff in best practices in literacy and data analysis; and to train the staff in the design, use, and evaluation of data folders. The use of data folders was a district priority that involved teachers keeping class-level and student-level records of students' assessment performance and progress on specific skills. The SLT also wanted to set up study groups for the third- and fifth-grade teachers to give these teachers an opportunity to collaboratively improve their instructional practices to better meet specific student learning needs.

The mini data retreat that was held after they returned allowed the entire staff to share in the process of identifying their students' most pressing instructional needs. A first-grade teacher who had never paid much attention to upper grades' achievement scores was surprised to discover that phonemic awareness was a weakness among third-grade students. She said, "That is something I should be teaching. Students shouldn't be leaving my class without that knowledge." Other teachers had similar revelations and were in many ways encouraged by the data analysis process. With improvement in some key areas, several concluded, they could significantly boost their scores.

Box A.4   Leadership Institute: Building Capacity to Lead High-Quality Professional Development

Schools and districts working with the Porter Center come together to participate in an intensive multiday leadership institute. The focus of the institute is on developing the knowledge and skills needed by leaders to plan, implement, monitor, and sustain high-quality professional development. Teams work with their coaches and other leadership institute faculty to apply their knowledge and skills to the development of a leadership action plan. Teams collaborate to build a deeper understanding of research-based professional development, evaluate professional development, sustain professional development focused on student achievement, and engage in processes for building professional learning communities. The goal is to build capacity to effectively lead high-quality professional development. The leadership institute equips teams to return to their sites ready to implement that plan and lead others in the creation of a comprehensive professional development system.

Year 2 (2003–2004)

Implementation

As the school began its second year of working with the Porter Center, the staff at Tibbott was ready to implement the first steps in their professional development plan. They had identified their highest priorities, which were to train all staff in best practices for literacy, to train and begin holding faculty study groups, and to train all staff in using data folders. Now they were ready to begin putting their plans into action.

Improving specific instructional areas. The data had shown that phonemic awareness was a weakness across the grade levels, so two staff members attended a conference and investigated various phonics programs. When they identified the program they thought would best meet their needs, the teachers presented it to the SLT. The principal approved it and found the money to fund it. This program is now in place and being used in all kindergarten and first-grade classrooms, although one aspect of it, having an aide, has been set aside because of budget priorities.

The data had also shown that making inferences while reading was a weakness in the third through fifth grades. To address this, they invited a district-level coordinator to train grade-level teams to implement CRISS strategies. CRISS stands for Creating Independence through Student-Owned Strategies. It is designed to help students in grades 4 through 12 read with more understanding by helping them to actively integrate new information with their prior knowledge.

Introducing data folders. Another important new initiative that they implemented during the second year proved to be helpful to Tibbott because it was aligned with the direction they were already taking. At the beginning of the year, a representative from the district came in to train the staff on the use of teacher and student data folders. Teachers expressed the usual concerns: Is this a good use of our time? Will this really improve student learning? Because many of them had already begun using individual assessment data to guide their instruction, however, the faculty on the whole embraced this new practice, albeit with some grumbling.

Forming study groups. Another professional development approach designed to support teachers as they implemented new strategies during the second year was teacher-led study groups in the third and fifth grade. These grades were selected because they were the grades being tested by the state of Illinois. The entire staff was given some training in how study groups work during a school-wide professional development day in September. The principal, coach, and a representative from the district were all there to answer questions about how study groups function effectively. At the initial study group meetings, the grade-level teams analyzed individual student data from their previous year's class to determine their own strengths and weaknesses instructionally. For example, after group members shared some of the results of this analysis, one veteran fifth-grade teacher decided to borrow some writing strategies from her less experienced colleagues because she could determine from the data that they were obtaining better results. At the same time, the newer teachers were eager to adopt some of her mental math problem-solving practices because her students had outperformed theirs in math.

Adopting a testing preparation program. One of the medium-priority items that the SLT had identified was to purchase Study Island, an online resource aligned with the Illinois learning standards designed to prepare students for the ISAT format and content, and train the third- and fifth-grade teachers to use it. In addition to allowing teachers and administrators to track individual student-, class-, and grade-level progress, the program focused teachers' attention on particular literacy skills. As a result of using this program, more teachers began tapping into their own data results and then adapting their instruction to meet individual student needs.

Continued coaching. During the second year, when staff members were implementing the literacy initiatives described previously and developing a professional development plan for math, the coach made four visits to the school and was available for numerous telephone conversations and e-mails. During these visits, she met with the SLT and visited classrooms to get a feel for how implementation was going. Were teachers using the new practices? Were they using new questioning strategies, data folders, and so on? She spent so much time in the school that even the students began to recognize her and greet her.

During these visits, the also spent much one-on-one time with the principal. They would meet over lunch for several hours, and she would listen to his concerns and help him focus his thoughts. The principal found these conversations helpful because they strengthened his conviction that the school was moving in the right direction, and they supported his decision to give more leadership responsibility to the SLT. He believed that the group was ready to take on more of a leadership role, but he also believed that if they were going to function effectively as schoolwide representatives and be credible with other staff members, then he needed to make sure that he maintained ultimate decision-making power. He viewed his job as supporting them while monitoring available resources and highest priorities.

The Current Picture (2004–2005)

Strengths Looking Forward

- *School climate is positive and focused on student achievement.* Everyone involved in the effort at Tibbott believes that the school is fundamentally different than it was before they began working with the Porter Center. The coach is astounded by their progress. She sat in on a recent meeting and listened to the SLT discuss where they needed to go with math instruction, and she was amazed at how much they knew. She stated, "They go as deep as you want them to go. When they are talking about fifth grade, they are immediately looking back to what happened in third grade. That's the kind of analysis they are comfortable with now."
  - One teacher mentioned that she truly believes that she is becoming the teacher she was meant to be after 27 years in the classroom. The principal reports that although there has not been universal implementation of all the new practices, "every person in the building has put more into making changes than ever before." Survey data collected at the end of Year 2 support the conclusion that a majority of Tibbott's teachers have a better attitude toward professional development and that they are using different practices as a result of the professional development initiatives. Ninety-five percent of the teachers agreed that staff attitudes had improved toward professional development; 87% reported that their instructional practices had changed as a result of one or more of the new initiatives.

- *Student-level data increasingly used to drive instruction.* A concrete example of this is teachers' use of data folders. Compiling classroom and individual student folders is now an expected practice across the district that is tied to teacher evaluation. Because of the data folders, not only are teachers keeping a running record of each student's progress on specific skills but also in many classes, students maintain their own individual folders to track their progress. In one first-grade classroom, students record their progress by listing their goals and action plans and then graphing their scores on a bar graph. In this system, all students know the benchmark they need to reach because it is highlighted on their bar graph. Based on their current skill level, students brainstorm a list of strategies with the teacher in one-on-one meetings. For example, students might decide to do extra at-home assignments or learn new vocabulary words to improve their reading fluency.

- *More teachers differentiating instruction.* Many teachers have changed their instructional and assessment practices after learning to analyze individual students' skills. For example, one teacher now develops multiple assessments rather than using one. Her role in the classroom has also shifted. She notes,

> In the past, I assigned groups in the beginning of the year, and students pretty much stayed there. Now, I am always looking for kids to advance. I used to accept interruptions during guided reading. Now students know that I am not going to answer their questions during that time. I had to give up feeling responsible for the whole group and trust students to work effectively on their own more.

- *Shared leadership approach to school governance.* Another striking aspect about Tibbott is teachers' confidence that they are moving in the right direction. The principal notes that the SLT is so eager to maintain their progress that they asked to participate in the interview process when he was hiring new teachers last spring, soon before his retirement. Their confidence extends to data analysis. In the past, the principal presented the achievement data to the staff each year when the data were released. This year, the former assistant principal, who has taken over as principal, reports that the teachers were so eager to dig into the 2004 data and find out how their students had scored that they analyzed the data themselves and brought the data to a faculty meeting as soon as the data were released. Recognizing the skills that staff members now possess, she intends to lead "collaboratively." She stated, "We are equipped to move ahead because every teacher understands and knows how to correctly analyze data." Several people on the staff and at the district expressed confidence that she would build on their success.

- *External recognition of the school's progress.* Tibbott's hard work has been recognized externally. Several teachers were invited to attend a workshop at Learning Point Associates to discuss their experience with a roundtable that included representatives from the U.S. Department of Education. The teachers were surprised at how valued and appreciated their insights were as they spoke about how they use data to inform their instruction. Not long after this, one of the first-grade teachers received a national award for teaching. The school also received an award from the South Suburban Illinois Association of Supervision and Curriculum Development for outstanding shared leadership at the building level.

- *Success meeting federal accountability goals.* Tibbott has made AYP 2 years in a row by boosting students' achievement scores in several key areas. For example, the percentage of Hispanic students in third grade who met or exceeded standards in reading increased from 43% in 2002 to 54% in 2004. During the course of the 2003–2004 school year, third-grade teachers who focused on improving students' ability to read and comprehend informational sources saw their pass rates increase from 58% to 72% in this area. Third-grade writing pass rates for the school as a whole increased from 55% to 67% between 2002 and 2004.

- *Continuing external assistance.* The Porter Center work at Tibbott is not over. The coach visited the school four times during the 2004–2005 school year to provide leadership coaching to the principal and ongoing support to the SLT as they began to implement some of their plans for math instruction. In addition to this work, the district turned to the Porter Center to help it find an external provider who could help them improve literacy instruction across the district. As a result, the Porter Center brokered a larger contract for Learning Point Associates to implement several years of literacy training. For Tibbott, this means that they will have a trusted partner to work with as they continue to refine and improve their literacy strategies.

Challenges Looking Forward

Despite all the good news at Tibbott, there are still major challenges:

- *Redistricting affects staff and students.* In 2005, a new elementary school opened, which resulted in some major changes at Tibbott. The school lost 40% of its faculty and approximately 200 students to the new school. In this shift, the majority of the bilingual students transferred, but these have been replaced by a new group of bilingual students with new challenges. At a meeting in September, the SLT spoke openly about the need to decide if they should be giving up some practices to replace them with new practices that better address the current student population. The capacity building of the past few years has equipped Tibbott to manage these changes more effectively, but there is still much change for the school to absorb.
- *Changes in leadership.* The school has also lost its principal, who retired. Fortunately, he has been replaced by a leader who clearly is interested in maintaining the current course and has strong staff support. Another leadership change took place at the district level when a new superintendent came in at the beginning of the 2003–2004 school year. The new superintendent is committed to improving instruction and visits classrooms almost daily, but there is always

a chance that he will mandate something that takes Tibbott in a different direction.

- *Uneven implementation of new practices.* Not all teachers agree that the new practices improve student achievement. A faculty survey distributed in the spring of 2004 found that 27% of the teachers did not think the information at the mini data retreat in September had been useful. Furthermore, 24% of the teachers do not want to continue to use student data folders, and 43% would like to discontinue using teacher data folders. To maintain their progress, the administration and the SLT will need to keep working on monitoring implementation and make sure teachers do not lose momentum.

- *Student achievement scores leave room for improvement.* The school also has a long way to go in both literacy and math achievement. Although Tibbott made AYP in 2004, overall only 54% of the students met or exceeded standards in reading. Among the subgroups, only 41% of Hispanic students met or exceeded standards in reading, and only 45% of black students did so. When the pass rate in Illinois to make AYP increases to 47.5% in 2006, Tibbott may have trouble getting all its subgroups up to this level. Math scores were higher in 2004, but overall, only 77% of all students met or exceeded standards in math.

- *Uncertainty about how Tibbott's experiences will influence the rest of the district.* Another unknown is what impact the changes at Tibbott will have on the rest of the district. At the beginning of this process, district administrators anticipated that they would leverage their investment in Tibbott by having the faculty and administration there become trainers for other schools. Although shared leadership has become a stronghold at Tibbott, the effort to spread their learning beyond the school has not yet been tapped by the district.

Resource B

High School Reform

It is apparent that high school is a viable reform issue. President George W. Bush proposed legislation to Congress in early 2005, but his plan did not receive much support. Congress was clearly more interested in reauthorizing the Carl D. Perkins Vocational and Technical Education Act for secondary vocational education than imposing more No Child Left Behind (NCLB) requirements on high schools. Despite the fact that President Bush's plan did not receive much support from representatives and senators, there were signs that changing high schools was going to be a priority of other leading policymakers and business executives.

The Bill and Melinda Gates Foundation is investing considerable funds to create a new model of high school in which all students feel well-known and supported. The foundation issued a report titled "High Schools for the New Millennium: Imagine the Possibilities" (www.gatesfoundation.org/nr/downloads/ed/edwhitepaper.pdf).

The National Governors' Association and Achieve sponsored the 2005 National Education Summit on High Schools. This summit was attended by governors, business executives, and K–12 educators. One result of the summit was the formation of the American Diploma Project network (ADP), with 13 states committing to raise their high school standards, assessments, and curriculum to align them with the demands of postsecondary education and work (www.achieve.org/achieve.nsf/2005Summit?OpenForm).

More states are making a commitment to the ADP network. As of late 2005, 21 states participating in ADP collectively educated 46% of the nation's high school students. The states participating in the diploma project are focusing on four key points:

- Raise high school standards to the level of what is actually required to succeed in college or the workforce
- Require all students to take rigorous college and work-ready curriculum
- Develop tests of college and work readiness that all students will take in high school
- Hold high schools accountable for graduating all students ready for college and work, and hold colleges responsible for the students they admit

In May 2005, the Institute of Education Sciences (IES) and Learning Point Associates (LPA) collaborated on a meeting specifically to focus on research to improve high schools called the Research on Improving High Schools: A Forum for Advancing the Research Agenda. The meeting preparation notebook included a comprehensive list of resources for high school reform work. That list is an example of an organized database of credible sources to use for high school reform activities. It is also organized in a manner that categorizes the information. This database is an excellent resource for a high school leadership committee working on reform planning.

Because the issue of high school reform has gained momentum with so many policymakers and business leaders, a partial list of the important topics and supporting reports from the IES/LPA forum is included here. A complete list of the research papers and additional information from the forum can be found on the Center for High School Excellence Web site at www.chse.org/policy/may5.php.

U.S. Department of Education Research and Reports

Education Longitudinal Studies

The Education Longitudinal Studies provide in-depth, student-based information on representative samples of U.S. students as they progress from secondary schooling to subsequent education and work roles.

High School and Beyond
http://nces.ed.gov/surveys/hsb

The National Center for Education Statistics (NCES) initiated a second longitudinal study, High School and Beyond (HS&B), to complement the first, the National Longitudinal Study of the High School Class of 1972 (NLS-72). HS&B studied the high school students of 1980, attempting to collect the same type of data gathered in NLS-72. The second study differed from the first in two significant ways, however. First, it addressed many newer issues of the educational process. Second, it included a sophomore cohort as well as a senior cohort. Adding the sophomore cohort made it possible to study high school dropouts and analyze changes and processes during high school. The base-year survey of HS&B and the follow-up surveys have addressed the issues of educational attainment, employment, family formation, personal values, and community activities since 1980.

National Assessment of Educational Progress
National Center for Education Statistics
http://nces.ed.gov/nationsreportcard/

The National Assessment of Educational Progress (NAEP) provides nationally and regionally representative information to track changes over time in achievement for 4th-, 8th-, and 12th-grade students in mathematics, reading, science, and other content domains. It also provides breakouts in performance for demographic subgroups and collects some other information to demonstrate relationships between performance and other measures. NAEP also provides state representative information on student achievement in public schools in limited domains and grade levels.

Program for International Student Assessment
National Center for Education Statistics
http://nces.ed.gov/surveys/pisa and www.pisa.oecd.org

The Program for International Student Assessment (PISA) is sponsored by the Organization for Economic Cooperation and Development. PISA is designed to monitor, on a regular 3-year cycle, the achievement of 15-year-old students in three subject areas: reading literacy, mathematical literacy, and scientific literacy. Although some elements covered by PISA are likely to be part of the school curriculum, PISA goes beyond mastery of a defined body of school-based knowledge to include the knowledge and experiences gained outside of school. In each assessment cycle (assessment cycles began in 2000), PISA focuses on one of three subject areas, devoting approximately two thirds of testing time to an in-depth assessment of the major domain and the remaining one third of testing time to the other two minor domains. In the United States, a nationally representative sample of 15-year-old students are asked to complete the PISA assessment. In addition, background questionnaires are administered in each participating country. To assess the performance of students and to provide education-related contextual information to understand their performance, PISA includes the following three components: assessment items, student questionnaire, and a school questionnaire for school administrators.

U.S. Department of Education Evaluations

Analysis of Advanced Placement Participation and Performance
Policy and Program Studies Service
Contact: Michael Fong at michael.fong@ed.gov

This is a 1-year study of advanced placement (AP) participation and performance by the nation's public school students. The U.S.

Department of Education is required to submit annual performance data from its two federal AP grant programs under NCLB. To address these requirements, this study compiles national and state-level results of the number of AP exams taken in high schools as a percentage of high school enrollment and the distribution of AP exam scores. Wherever possible, results are disaggregated by student characteristics and by AP exam.

Implementation Study of the Smaller Learning Communities Program
  Policy and Program Studies Service
  Contact: James Maxwell at james.maxwell@ed.gov

The subject of this study is the implementation of projects funded under the U.S. Department of Education's Smaller Learning Communities (SLC) program. This study provides program implementation information and will provide information on program impact. The study examines how schools are implementing the SLC program and how program implementation and outcomes vary by approach and type of school. ABT is the contractor for the study.

National Assessment of Vocational Education
  Policy and Program Studies Service
  www.ed.gov/rschstat/eval/sectech/nave/index.html (home page) www.ed.gov/rschstat/eval/sectech/nave/reports.html (reports)

The National Assessment of Vocational Education (NAVE) is a periodic, congressionally mandated study that examines the implementation and effects of federal vocational education policy. Responding to current policy issues, recent evaluations have examined topics such as increased emphasis on academic reform and college preparation. The latest NAVE, completed in 2004, examined the status of vocational education throughout the country and evaluated the impact of changes in the Carl D. Perkins Vocation and Technical Education Act of 1998 (also known as Perkins III).

U.S. Department of Education Reports

Dual Credit and Exam-Based Courses in U.S. Public High Schools: 2002–03 (2005)
National Center for Education Statistics
http://nces.ed.gov/pubsearch/pubsinfo.asp?pubid=2005009
This is the first national survey to provide baseline data for public high school students on dual-credit and exam-based courses, including AP and international baccalaureate courses. The report provides national estimates of participating schools and of the student enrollment in these courses. Survey findings are presented at the national level and by school characteristics, such as enrollment size, school locale, region, and percentage of minority enrollment.

Dual Enrollment of High School Students at Postsecondary Institutions: 2002–03 (2005)
National Center for Education Statistics
http://nces.ed.gov/pubsearch/pubsinfo.asp?pubid=2005008
This report provides data from a nationally representative survey of postsecondary institutions on the topic of dual enrollment of high school students. Survey findings are presented at the national level and by institution type and size. Survey respondents provided descriptive information about their dual-enrollment programs and about the prevalence of college course taking by high school students at their institutions during the 2002–2003 school year.

Policies and Practices

College Readiness and Rigor

Advanced Placement Report to the Nation (2005)
College Board
www.collegeboard.com/about/news_info/ap/2005/
This report presents a new measure of AP equity and excellence: the percentage of students in a school, district, or state who had at least one AP experience that resulted in an exam score of

3 or higher. This measure will provide information about access to AP courses and success on AP exams in schools and districts throughout the nation.

On Course for Success: A Close Look at Selected High School Courses That Prepare All Students for College (2004)
ACT, Incorporated and The Education Trust
www.act.org/path/policy/pdf/success_report.pdf
This study is based on an analysis of data from 10 schools. These schools were selected because they had significant enrollments of low-income or minority students or both who performed well on ACT subject tests. The authors found that successful students were enrolled in college preparatory courses, teachers were well qualified, teachers used a variety of instructional approaches, and tutorial support was provided for students.

Rising to the Challenge: Are High School Graduates Prepared for College and Work? (2005).
Achieve, Incorporated
www.achieve.org/dstore.nsf/Lookup/pollreport/$file/poll-report.pdf
This study analyzes the results of a December 2004 survey for which public high school graduates, employers, and college instructors were interviewed. Nearly 40% of high school graduates noted gaps between the education they received in high school and the skills that they are expected to have in college or the workplace. Moreover, more than 40% of college instructors and employers found that students were not prepared for college-level classes or jobs beyond the entry level.

Ready or Not: Creating a High School Diploma That Counts (2004).
American Diploma Project
www.achieve.org/dstore.nsf/Lookup/ADPreport/$file/ADPreport.pdf
This report stresses the importance of high standards to ensure that high school diplomas have value. The authors worked with representatives from higher education and the workforce to

determine the skills and knowledge that high school graduates must have to succeed in postsecondary education or the world of work. On the basis of this consensus, the authors created a series of concrete benchmarks that will prepare students for high school graduation and presented them in this user-friendly document. The America Diploma Project urges state policymakers to use these benchmarks to guide the creation of a system of assessments and graduation requirements that will prepare students for college and work.

Standards for What? The Economic Roots of K–16 Reform (2003)
Carnevale and Desrochers
acrnetwork.org/ViewDoc.aspx?ID=600076
This report is based on the authors' analysis of labor and demographic data. As the baby boomers retire and the information-based economy increases the demand for highly skilled workers, there will be a significant shortage of skilled workers in the future. Thus, the authors argue that it is essential to improve the quality of high school education to maintain the economic competitiveness of the United States. State policymakers must align standards and curricula to postsecondary education and labor market requirements. The curriculum must integrate academic and applied curricula to ensure that students have both a solid academic foundation and well-developed skills in problem solving, critical thinking, and interpersonal communication.

Education and Skills for the 21st Century: An Agenda for Action (2005)
Jobs for the Future
www.jff.org/jff/PDFDocuments/ActionAgenda.pdf
This brief document outlines the reasons why high schools have to change dramatically to prepare students for the demands of the information-based economy of the 21st century. To meet these challenges, educational institutions will need to accelerate achievement and learning for all students and promote lifelong learning. The authors outline action steps for employers, secondary

schools, institutions of higher education, and state and federal governments.

Exit Exams

Do Graduation Tests Measure Up? A Closer Look at State High School Exit Exams (2004)
Achieve, Incorporated
www.achieve.org/dstore.nsf/Lookup/TestGraduation-FinalReport/$file/TestGraduation-FinalReport.pdf

Achieve analyzed the rigor of exit exams in six states—Florida, Maryland, Massachusetts, New Jersey, Ohio, and Texas—and concluded that these exams, in isolation, set a low bar for achievement in these states. The report recommends three important changes that should be phased in over time. First, the exams should incorporate more challenging material from the entire high school curriculum. Second, the exams should include more challenging questions and cut scores should be set higher. Third, states and districts must develop a range of high-quality assessments that will contribute to high school graduation requirements.

Graduation Requirements, Graduation Rates, and Dropout Rates

The Expectations Gap: A 50-State Review of High School Graduation Requirements (2004)
Achieve, Incorporated
www.achieve.org/dstore.nsf/Lookup/coursetaking/$file/coursetaking.pdf

This report reviews the graduation requirements of all 50 states and concludes that no state requires the courses necessary for success in postsecondary education and work.

Locating the Dropout Crisis: Which High Schools Produce the Nation's Dropouts? Where Are They Located? Who Attends Them? (2004)
Balfanz and Legters
www.csos.jhu.edu/tdhs/rsch/Locating_Dropouts.pdf

This report analyzes current issues surrounding the high school dropout problem in the United States. The authors examine the number of freshmen versus the number of seniors 4 years later to determine what they call "promoting power." Findings from this analysis include the following: Promoting power in 20% of U.S. high schools is weak; overwhelmingly, these high schools have high percentages of minority student populations; and a relatively small number of U.S. cities have the weakest promoting power, which makes it nearly impossible for some students to attend a high school other than one with weak promoting power.

The Dropout Crisis: Promising Approaches in Prevention and Recovery (2004)
Steinberg and Almeida
www.jff.org/jff/PDFDocuments/dropoutcrisis.pdf
This report examines the high school dropout problem and identifies strategies for preventing dropouts and for reconnecting with those students who have dropped out. The document also gives states advice on how to address the dropout crisis and provides guidance on developing a stronger system of options for young people.

Federal Policy

Left Out and Left Behind: NCLB and the American High School (2003)
Joftus and Maddox-Dolan
www.all4ed.org/publications/NCLB/NCLB.pdf
This report discusses NCLB requirements for high schools. It also describes the provisions of the 10 state accountability plans approved by the U.S. Department of Education as of April 2003, when this document was published.

High School Redesign Strategies

Redesigning the American High School (2004)
National Governors Association
www.nga.org

This initiative is a joint effort of the National Governors' Association Center for Best Practices, Achieve, the National Conference of State Legislatures, and Jobs for the Future. Its Web site provides information about the national initiative and about what governors throughout the nation are doing to improve the quality of education in their states. The organizations involved will consult with individual states to advance statewide high school improvement efforts. In February 2005, the National Governors' Association and Achieve hosted the National Education Summit on High Schools. Materials from the summit are available at www .nga.org.

Advancing High School Reform in the States: Policies and Programs (2005)

Martinez, M.

http://www.kwfdn.org/resource_library/_resources/Advacing_hs.pdf

Martinez describes a variety of promising state policies and programs related to the following reform strategies: increased academic rigor, personalized instruction, supports for low-performing students, improving literacy skills, assessments, school leadership, highly qualified teachers, and providing assistance for high schools identified as in need of improvement.

A Call to Action: Transforming High School for All Youth (2005)
National High School Alliance
www.hsalliance.org

The National High School Alliance recommends a series of strategies related to six core principles for high school reform: personalized learning environments; academic engagement of all students; empowered educators; accountable leaders; engaged community and youth; and an integrated system of high standards, curriculum, instruction, assessments, and supports.

Accelerating Advancement in School and Work (2003)
Pennington
www.jff.org/jff/PDFDocuments/Pennbep.pdf

This publication argues that the transition from high school to college or careers must be radically redesigned to create a system of multiple pathways through which students will master a set of common high standards but through different types of institutions and in different amounts of time. Policymakers should create a wide range of high-quality educational options that provide a system of supports and interventions to ensure that all students succeed. To support these options, policymakers will have to set high standards and clear accountability measures; align funding streams; develop new governance models; build the capacity of teachers; increase the rigor of the curriculum; and strengthen connections between high schools, postsecondary options, and the community.

Breaking Ranks II: Strategies for Leading High School Reform (2004)
National Association of Secondary School Principals
http://nasspcms.principals.org/s_nassp/sec.asp?CID=563&DID=48223

The National Association of Secondary School Principals has created a practical guide to lead high school principals through a process of needs assessment and a series of action steps to implement 31 recommended high school reforms in three core areas: collaborative leadership and professional learning communities; personalization; and curriculum, instruction, and assessment. The authors outline seven strategies that must be addressed to improve educational outcomes for students: core knowledge and skills, connections between students and adults, personalized planning, differentiated curriculum, flexible use of time, distributed leadership, and continuous professional development. The report contains user-friendly tools, references, resources, and a number of school profiles that illustrate the recommended high school reforms in practice. See also the Janice Ollarvia webcast, "What's Needed for High School Principals to 'Break Ranks'?" (www.nccte .org/webcasts/description.asp?wc=146).

Rigorous Research

Is There Solid Evidence of Positive Effects for High School Students? (2004)

Stern and Wing

http://casn.berkeley.edu/resources/solid_evidence.html

The authors examine three studies that have produced positive impacts for high school students. The research methodology for each study is strong, with each using random assignment. The authors suggest that the rigorous evaluation methods used in these three studies also need to be applied to other interventions to determine their impact on high school students. The first study, which examined the Quantum Opportunity Program, indicated that the program significantly increased high school completion rates and resulted in additional positive outcomes. The second study, which examined Upward Bound, found that participants who had not expected to earn bachelor's degrees significantly increased their rate of 4-year college attendance. The third study, which examined career academies, revealed that academy students reported receiving more support while in high school, were more likely to combine academic and technical courses, and were more likely to work in jobs connected to school. Four years after scheduled graduation, there was no difference in educational attainment between the control and academy student groups, but there was a significant impact on employment and earnings for academy students.

Making Progress Toward Graduation: Evidence From the Talent Development High School Model

This report describes the Talent Development model and its implementation in five low-performing high schools in Philadelphia. MDRC used strong quasi-experimental methods to evaluate the impact of the program on three cohorts of students. Many Talent Development schools place freshmen in smaller learning communities to ease their transition into high school and improve their academic preparation. As a result, in Philadelphia, first-time 9th graders achieved substantial gains in attendance, academic course credits, and promotion rates during their first year in high school. The improvements in credits earned and promotion rates were sustained as these students progressed through high school. The model also produced improvements in high school graduation rates and mathematics test scores for 11th graders. Although these schools still have a great deal of room for improvement, the results of this study are encouraging.

References

Achieve. (1999). *National Education Summit briefing book.* Washington, DC: Author.

Achieve. (2001). *National Education Summit briefing book.* Washington, DC: Author.

Adelman, N. E. (Project Director.). (1996, October). *The uses of time for teaching and learning,* ORAD 96-1323. Washington, DC: U.S. Department of Education, Office of Education Research and Improvement.

Alvarado, A. (2005, January). Banking on teachers. *Education Update, 47*(1), 1.

American Association of School Administrators. (n.d.). *Using data to improve schools—What's working.* Arlington, VA: Author.

American heritage dictionary of the English language. (1975). New York: Houghton Mifflin.

Balfanz, R., & Legters, N. (2004). Locating the dropout crisis: Which high schools produce the nation's dropouts? Where are they located? Who attends them? Baltimore: Johns Hopkins University Press.

Big blue's bold step into China. (2004, December 20). *Business Week,* 35–36.

Black, P., Harrison, C., Lee, C., Marshall, B., & Wiliam, D. (1998). *Working inside the black box: Assessment for learning in the classroom.* London: King's College of London.

Black, P., & Wiliam, D. (1998). *Inside the black box—Raising standards through classroom assessment.* London: King's College of London.

Carnevale, A., & Desrochers, D. (2003). *Standards for what? The economic roots of K–16 reform.* Washington, DC: Educational Testing Service.

Chaddock, G. (1998, August 25). Perils of the pendulum: Resisting education fads. *The Christian Science Monitor.* Retrieved from http://www.csmonitor.com.

Collins, J. (2001). *Good to great.* Boston: Harvard Business School Press.

Crisis in American education. (1958, March 31). *Life,* 93–100.

Crowther, F., Kaagan, S., Ferguson, M., & Hann, L. (2002). *Developing teacher leaders.* Thousand Oaks, CA: Corwin Press.

Easton, L. (2004, August/September). Process—Selecting the strategy that works for your context and content. *Tools for schools, 1.*

Elmore, R. (2005, Spring). School improvement requires new knowledge, not just good will. *American Educator, 27.*

Freedman, S. (2004, September 29). Politics aside, a school's real success. *New York Times.* Retrieved from http://www.nytimes.com

Fullan, M., Bertani, L., & Quinn, J. (2004, April). New lessons for districtwide reform. *Educational Leadership, 61*(7), 42–46.

Gawande, A. (2002). *Complications: A surgeon's notes on an imperfect science.* New York: Metropolitan Books/Holt.

Gerstner, L., Jr. (2002). *Who says elephants can't dance? Inside IBM's historic turnaround.* New York: HarperCollins.

Glanz, J. (1998). *Action research: An educational leader's guide to school improvement.* Norwood, MA: Christopher-Gordon.

Goldberg, M., & Cross, C. T. (2005, October). Time and learning—A new introduction. In *Prisoners of time* (Rev. ed., p. 2). Washington, DC: National Education Commission on Time and Learning. Retrieved from http://www.ecs.org/clearinghouse/64/52/6452.pdf

Guskey, T. (2000). *Evaluating professional development.* Thousand Oaks, CA: Corwin Press.

Henke, K. (2005, December/January). The data game. *Scholastic Administrator,* 45–48.

Hiebert, J., & Stigler, J. (1999). *The teaching gap.* New York: Free Press.

James, F. (2004, December 4). Bush picks for cabinet have shared trait. *Chicago Tribune,* p. 1.

Joftus, S., & Maddox-Dolan, B. (2003). *Left out and left behind: NCLB and the American high school.* Washington, DC: Alliance for Excellent Education.

Kaiser, R. (2005, May 24). Focus on schools helps Finns build a showcase nation. *The Washington Post,* p. A12.

Kimmelman, P., & Kroeze, D. (2002). *Achieving world-class schools: Mastering school improvement using a genetic model.* Norwood, MA: Christopher-Gordon.

King, J. (2005, January 23). Indian Hill School's award nomination a much needed lift. *Daily Herald.* Retrieved from http://www.daily herald.com

Kocour, R. (with Hodgson, M.). (1998). *Facing the extreme.* New York: St. Martin's.

Kotter, J., & Cohen, D. (2002). *The heart of change.* Boston: Harvard Business School Press.

Krakauer, J. (1997). *Into thin air.* New York: Anchor.

Learning Point Associates. (2001). *Data retreat participant's guide.* Naperville, IL: Author.

Lewis, M. (2003). *Moneyball: The art of winning an unfair game.* New York: Norton.

Martinez, M. (2005). *Advancing high school reform in the states: Policies and programs.* Reston, VA: National Association of Secondary School Principals.

McEwan, E., & McEwan, P. (2003). *Making sense of research: What's good, what's not, and how to tell the difference.* Thousand Oak, CA: Corwin Press.

McGehee, T. (2001). *Whoosh.* Cambridge, MA: Perseus.

Mills, L. (2005, September). Show me the data. *School Administrator, 62*(8), 8.

Morrell, M., & Capparell, S. (2001). *Shackelton's way.* New York: Penguin.

National Commission on Teaching and America's Future. (1996). *What matters most: Teaching for America's future.* New York: Author.

National Education Commission on Time and Learning. (1994, April). *Prisoners of time.* Washington, DC: Author.

National Staff Development Council. (2004). *Powerful designs for professional learning.* Oxford, OH: Author.

Neilsen, J. (with Vollers, M.). (2001). *Ice bound—A doctor's incredible battle for survival at the South Pole.* New York: Hyperion.

Neville, K., Rachel, S., Sherman, H., & Carol, E. (2005). *Preparing and training professionals: Comparing education and six other fields.* Washington, DC: The Finance Project.

No Child Left Behind Act of 2001. (2001). Conference report to accompany H.R.1, Dec 13 (legislative day, December 12). Ordered to be printed, 107th Congress, 1st Session, House of Representatives, Report 107-334. Washington, DC: U.S. Government Printing Office.

Olson, L. (2005). ETS to enter formative assessment market at K-12 level. *Education Week, 24*(25), 11.

Pennington, H. (2003). Accelerating advancement in school and work. In D. Ravitch (Ed.), *Brookings papers on education policy: 2003* (pp. 339–376). Washington, DC: Brookings Institution Press.

Rasmussen, C., Hopkins, S., & Fitzpatrick, M. (2004, Winter). Our work done well is like the perfect pitch. *Journal of Staff Development, 25*(1), 16–25.

Richardson, V. (2003, January). The dilemmas of professional development. *Phi Delta Kappan, 84*(5), 401–406.

Schwarz, A. (2004). *The numbers game—Baseball's lifelong fascination with statistics* (p. ix). New York: Dunne/St. Martin's.

Senge, P. (1990). *The fifth discipline.* New York: Doubleday.

Shavelson, R., & Towne, L. (Eds.). (2002). *Scientific research in education.* Washington, DC: National Academy Press, Committee on Scientific Principles for Education Research.

Shek, K. (2005, August 25). Public views high schools as focus for reform efforts. *Education Daily, 38*(152), 1.

60 Minutes. (2005, January 2). [Television broadcast]. New York: CBS Broadcasting.

Steinberg, A., & Almeida, C. (2004). *The dropout crisis: Promising approaches in prevention and recovery.* Boston: Jobs for the Future.

Steiner, L. (2004). *Designing effective professional development experiences; What do we know* (2nd ed.). Naperville, IL: Learning Point Associates.

Stern, D., & Wing, J. Y. (2004). *Is there solid evidence of positive effects for high school students?* Berkeley: University of California Press.

Tiwana, A. (2000). *The knowledge management toolkit.* Upper Saddle River, NJ: Prentice Hall.

Tobin, J. (2003). *To conquer the air—The Wright brothers and the great race for flight.* New York: Free Press.

Towne, L., Wise, L. L., & Winters, T. M. (Eds.). (2005). *Advancing scientific research in education* Washington, DC: National Academies Press.

Trotter, A. (2005, February 16). Tool helps Washington teachers write learning plans. *Education Week,* 6.

U.S. Department of Education, National Commission on Excellence in Education. (1983). *A nation at risk.* Washington, DC: Author.

U.S. Department of Education, National Commission on Mathematics and Science Teaching for the 21st Century. (2000, September). *Before it's too late—A report to the nation from the National Commission on Mathematics and Science Teaching for the 21st Century.* Washington, DC: Author.

U.S. Department of Education, Office of the Undersecretary. (2000). *Does professional development change teaching practice? Results from a three-year study* (Document No. 2000-04). Washington, DC: Author.

Walton, M. (1991). *Deming management at work.* New York: Perigee.

Welch, J. (with Byrne, J.). (2001). *Jack.* New York: Warner.

Welch, J. (with Welch, S.). (2005). *Winning.* New York: Harper.

White, M. (1987). *The Japanese educational challenge: A commitment to children.* New York/London: Free Press/Collier Macmillan.

Whitehurst, G. (2002, March 5). *Research on teacher preparation and professional development,* White House Conference on Preparing Tomorrow's Teachers. Washington, DC: U.S. Department of Education.

Index

A

Accelerating Advancement in School and Work, 159–160

Accountability
challenges of, 58, 70
importance of, 22, 89, 110
internal, 95
laws, 91–92
meeting requirements of, 72, 115–117
strengthening, 16–17
teacher, 121

Achieve, Incorporated, 155, 157

Achievement gap, 7, 20–21

Achievement. *See* Assessment; Student performance

Achieving World-Class Schools, 97

ACT, Incorporated, 155

Action ideas, 24–25, 63–64, 89–90

Adequate yearly progress (AYP)
defined, 40
determining, 29
failing to meet, 2, 43, 46
role of teachers in, 73
safe harbor and, 46
state, 121, 122
stoplight reports, 84–85 (figure), 86 (figure)
subjects not tested for, 33
tools for achieving, 77

Advanced Placement Report to the Nation, 154–155

Advancing High School Reform in the States, 159

Advancing Scientific Research in Education, 51

Alliance for Excellent Education, 25

Almeida, C., 158

Alvarado, Anthony, 93

American Association of School Administrators, 1–2

American Diploma Project network (ADP), 149–150, 155–156

American Educational Research Association (AERA), 64

American Institutes for Research, 65

Analysis of Advanced Placement Participation and Performance, 152–153

Arndt, Ken, 109–113

Assessment
formative, 73–75, 120
international, 28, 126
nationally normed, 38, 41, 73
problems with, 40
state, 37–38, 43, 73, 80
tools, 76–88
See also Student performance

B

Balfanz, R., 157–158
Bell, Terrell, 7
Bertani, A. L., 106–106
Bill and Melinda Gates
    Foundation, 149
Boehner, John, 128
*Breaking Ranks II: Strategies for
    Leading High School Reform,* 160
Burkhardt, Gina, 119
Bush, President George H. W.,
    9, 12–13
Bush, President George H. W., 20,
    22, 25, 116, 128, 149

C

*Call to Action, Transforming High
    School for All Youth,* 159
Carl D. Perkins Vocation and
    Technical Education Act,
    149, 153
Carnevale, A., 156
Case studies, 97, 98, 120–123,
    129–147
Chaddock, Gail Russell, 49
Clinton, President William J.,
    9, 12–13
Coaching, 123
Cohen, Dan, 47, 70
College Board, 154–155
College readiness, 154–157
Collins, Jim, 42, 44
Council of Chief State School
    Officers, 65
Crowther, F., 104
Curriculum, 125–126

D

Data
    accessing, 43–44, 62, 109–113, 126
    acquisition. *See* Knowledge
        acquisition
    analyzing, 35, 37–46, 120

    disaggregated assessment, 21,
        22, 31, 40, 45
    hypotheses about, 41, 45–46
    importance of, 35, 38–43, 62,
        68–70, 82, 91, 126
    improvement goals and, 41, 46
    management. *See* Knowledge
        management
    reliability of, 44
    retreats, 40–47, 62
    using, 29, 32, 35–40
    See also Knowledge acquisition;
        Knowledge management;
        Research
Deming, W. Edwards, 36
DesCartes, 76
Desrochers, D., 156
*Do Graduation Tests Measure
    Up?,* 157
Doyle, Denis, ix
Dropout Crisis, The, 158
Dropout rates, 157–158
*Dual Credit and Exam-Based Courses
    in U.S. Public High Schools,* 154
*Dual Enrollment of High School
    Students at Postsecondary
    Institutions,* 154

E

*Education and Skills for the 21st
    Century,* 156–157
Education Commission of the
    States, 12, 65
Education costs, 3, 5, 6, 96,
    111–112, 120
Education Council Act of 1991, 10
Education reform
    challenges of, 113, 115–117, 119
    costs, 111–112
    districtwide, 105–106, 109–113
    effective, 91, 111, 120–123
    efforts, 5–24
    global community and, 108–109

high school. *See* High school reform
outside contractors, 111, 121
public support for, 20
school culture, 2, 70, 88
superintendent role in, 109–113, 119
versus business, 13–14, 96
See also School improvement plans
Education Sciences Reform Act, 49
Education Testing Service, 65, 75
Education Trust, The, 65, 155
Eisenhower, President Dwight, 5
Electronic Individual Learning Plan (EILP), 72, 77–81 (figure), 126
Elementary and Secondary Education Act (ESEA), 6–7, 13
Elmore, Richard, 95
Evaluation, 42, 47. *See also* Assessment
Evidence-based information, 35, 48–50, 61, 69. *See also* Data; Research
Exit exams, 157

F
Farley, Karen, 80
Federal role in education, 3, 5–6, 8–21, 22, 158. *See also* U.S. Department of Education
Ferguson, M., 104
Finance Project, The, 96
First in the World Consortium, 27, 31, 125–126
Fitzpatrick, M., 99
Fullan, M., 105–106

G
Gerstner, Louis, Jr., 13, 118
Glanz, J., 103

Glen Commission. *See* National Commission on Mathematics and Science Teaching
Glenn, John, 17
Goals 2000, 12–13
Good to Great, 42
Google, 71
Graduation requirements/rates, 157–158
Great Society program, 6
Gregg, Judd, 128
Grounded intuition, 32
Gusky, Tom, 102, 104

H
Hann, L., 104
Henke, Karen Greenwood, 38
Hiebert, James, 101
High Objective Uniform State Standards of Evaluation (HOUSSE), 23
High School and Beyond (HS&B), 151
High school reform
legislation initiative for, 25, 149
poll on, 25
programs, 149–150
research/reports on, 150–162
resources for, 150–162
viability of, 149
See also Education reform
High Schools for the New Millennium, 149
Himanen, Pekka, 100
Hopkins, S., 99

I
Illiteracy, 8
Implementation Study of the Smaller Learning Communities Program, 153
Individual education plans, 77–81, 123

Inside the Black Box, 75
Institute of Education Sciences (IES),
   23, 49–50, 63, 107, 120, 150
Instructional management
   solutions (IMS), 82–88
Intervention strategies, 72, 73–74
Is There Solid Evidence of Positive
   Effects for High School
   Students?, 161

J
Jobs for the Future, 156–157
Joftus, S., 158
John Edward Porter Professional
   Development Center, 97,
   129–130
Johnson, President Lyndon B., 6

K
Kaagan, S., 104
Kennedy, Edward, 128
Kirk, Mark, xxvi
Knowledge
   acquisition. *See* Knowledge
      acquisition
   defining, 31–32
   implementation. *See* Knowledge
      implementation
   importance of, 31–32, 88–89
   management. *See* Knowledge
      management
   model, 34, 35–36 (figure), 93,
      100, 115, 120, 125–128
   school improvement and, 31–34
   teacher. *See* Teachers,
      qualifications of
Knowledge acquisition
   action ideas for, 63–64
   analyzing data. *See* Data,
      analyzing
   building organizational capacity
      with. *See* Organizational
      capacity

   collection and organization,
      41, 43
   data/research for, 35, 37, 106,
      109, 120. *See also* Data;
      Research
   identifying performance points
      with, 36–37
   importance of, 29, 32–34,
      40, 62, 125
   model, 36 (figure), 88
   problems with, 38
   sustaining success with, 35–36
   See also Data; Knowledge
      implementation;
      Knowledge management
Knowledge implementation
   defined, 94
   importance of, 32–34, 91–92,
      97, 106, 125–127
   leadership and. *See* Leadership
   ongoing nature of, 93
   See also Knowledge acquisition;
      Professional development
Knowledge management
   challenges of, 71, 126
   defined, 67, 88
   importance of, 32, 34, 63,
      67–71, 75, 89, 125
   products, 75–81
   software, 90, 121
   solutions, 82–88
   See also Knowledge acquisition;
      Knowledge implementation
Knowledge Management Toolkit, 32
Kocour, Ruth Anne, 118
Kotter, John, 46, 47, 70
Krajenta, Marilyn, 63
Krakauer, Jon, 118

L
Leadership
   authentic, 123
   by superintendents, 109–113

by teachers. *See* Teachers, as leaders
districtwide reform, 105–106
examples of, 118, 119
importance of, 42, 93
professional development. *See* Professional development, leadership
teams, 41. *See also* Team work
Learning Point Associates, 41, 77, 97, 150
Left Out and Left Behind: NCLB and the American High School, 158
Legters, N., 157–158
Lesson study, 101–102
Lewis, Michael, 68–69
Life magazine, 6, 18
Little, Grady, 69, 88
Locating the Dropout Crisis, 157–158

M
Maddox-Dolan, B., 158
Making Progress Toward Graduation, 161–162
Making Sense of Research, 60
Martinez, M., 159
Math achievement. *See* Student performance, science and math
McCollough, Shawn Arevalo, 61
McEwan, E., 60–61
McEwan, P., 60–61
McGehee, Tom, 39, 119
McKinley Elementary School case study, 120–123
MDRC, 65
Measures of Academic Progress (MAP), 76–78 (figure), 79 (figure), 126
Medical model, 72
Miller, George, 128
Mills, Lane, 89–90

N
Nation at Risk, A, 7–9, 11, 19
National Academies, The, 64
National Assessment of Educational Progress, 151–152
National Assessment of Vocational Education, 153–154
National Association of Secondary School Principals, 160
National Center for Education Research, 50
National Center for Education Statistics, 50, 151–152, 154
National Center for Evaluation and Regional Assistance, 50
National Center for Research on Evaluation, Standards, and Student Testing (CRESST), 64
National Commission on Excellence in Education, 7
National Commission on Mathematics and Science Teaching, 17–19
National Commission on Teaching and America's Future, 14–15
National Commission on Time and Learning, 10–12
National Defense Education Act (NDEA), 5
National Education Association, 1–2, 111
National Education Summit on High Schools, 149
National Education Summit, 1996, 13–14
National Education Summit, 1999, 15–17
National Education Summit, 2001, 19–21
National Governor's Association, 9, 149, 158–159
National High School Alliance, 159

National Research Council,
  51–52, 64
National Staff Development
  Council (NSDC), 65, 98
NCLB compliance
  100% rule, 116, 117, 119, 122, 127
  adequate yearly progress. *See*
    Adequate yearly progress
  challenges of, 115–117, 125
  example of, 120–123
  non, 22, 24, 43, 61, 67, 115, 122
  organizational capacity and,
    22, 35, 91
  state testing and, 120
  successful, 33, 35, 43, 91
  teachers and, 72. *See also*
    Teachers
NCLB, future of, 4–5, 25, 29,
  119–123, 127
NCLB, history of
  events leading up to, 1–4, 30
  finalizing, 20
  funding and, 5
  signing into law, 22
  versus earlier reform efforts,
    5–21, 23–24
NCLB, overview of, 22–24, 30
NCLB, response to, 1–4, 29–30, 127
NCLB, standards/requirements of
  assessment of. *See* Assessment
  challenges of, 115–117, 127–128
  consequences of not meeting.
    See NCLB compliance, non
  core, 32, 33–34, 44
  data and. *See* Data
  examples of, 8, 10
  research-based, 3, 21–22, 28,
    29–30, 32. *See also* Research
  setting, 22–23
  sharing, 22–23
  subgroups, 7
  teacher quality. *See* Teachers,
    qualifications of

Nielsen, Jerri, 117–118
No Child Left Behind Act.
  See NCLB
North Central Regional Education
  Laboratory, 28
Northwest Evaluation Association
  (NWEA), 72, 76–79, 126

O
Office of Education Research
  and Improvement, 23, 49
On Course for Success, 155
Organization for Economic
  Cooperation and
  Development, 152
Organizational capacity, building
  example of, 120–123
  importance of, 24, 29–40, 47,
    61, 91, 100, 120, 125, 128
  linear process of, 32
  model of, 68 (figure), 92 (model),
    93, 100, 115
  professional development and.
    See Professional
    development
  stakeholders in, 109
  See also Knowledge, model

P
Pennington, H., 159–160
Perry, Oliver Hazard, 11, 19
Policy and Program Studies
  Service, 153
President's Education Summit,
  9–10
Professional development
  activities, 100–104, 109–113
  capacity building, 99–100. *See
    also* Organizational capacity,
    building
  case studies, 97, 98
  challenges of, 21, 94, 97,
    108–113

communities/groups, 100–103,
    120, 121, 123
funding for, 6, 96, 111–112, 120
goals of, 33, 100, 107–108
implementation and, 91, 93–100
importance of, 21, 91, 95–98, 100,
    106–113, 127
leadership, 33, 93, 104–106, 112
mentoring, 104, 110–111, 122
models, 102, 104, 107
ongoing, 21, 109–113
planning, 77, 100, 107–108
recommendations for, 96,
    98–100, 108–109
research-based, 6, 30, 33, 93–94,
    98–103, 108, 120, 123, 127
Program for International Student
    Assessment (PISA), 152
Program for Student Assessment
    (PISA), 3

Q
Quinn, J., 105–106

R
RAND Corporation, The, 65
Rasmussen, C., 99, 100
*Ready or Not: Creating a High
    School Diploma That Counts,*
    155–156
Reagan, President Ronald, 9
*Redesigning the American High
    School,* 158–159
Regional educational
    laboratories, 63
Remedial education, 8
Research
    action, 103
    credible, 28, 35, 48–50, 53, 62,
        106
    defined, 49
    federal. *See* U.S. Department of
        Education, research

high school, 150–162
knowledge acquisition and. *See*
    Knowledge acquisition,
    data/research for
longitudinal studies,
    151–152
math and science, 54–60, 107
model for, 60–61
NCLB, requirements and.
    See NCLB, standards/
    requirements of,
    research-based
professional development. *See*
    Professional development,
    research-based
recommendations for, 51–52
sources of, 28, 49–56, 62–63
using, 61, 67–70, 91, 108
versus intuition, 68–69
See also Data; Knowledge
    acquisition
Richardson, Virginia, 108
Riley, Richard, 13, 17
Rising to the Challenge, 155

S
Safe harbor provision, 46
Sanctions for non-compliance.
    See NCLB compliance, non
Saturn Corporation, 111
Saxon Math program, 54–60
School administration,
    non-traditional, 30–31
School choice, 118
School culture. *See* Education
    reform, school culture
School improvement plans
    continuous, 35–36, 92–95
    core structures of, 97
    data retreats and. *See* Data,
        retreats
    goals for, 39, 46, 122
    NCLB model for, 47

professional development and.
    See Professional
    development
reinventing the wheel in, 92
research-based, 108
See also Education reform
SchoolNet, 72, 82–83 (figure),
    84–85 (figure), 86 (figure), 87
    (figure), 88 (figure), 89
    (figure), 126
Schwarz, A., 69
Scientific Research in Education, 51
Senge, Peter, 57–59
September 11 terrorist
    attacks, 19
Shackleton, Ernest, 117
Soviet Union, 3, 5–6
Sparks, Dennis, 98
Specialized learning communities,
    56–59
Sputnik, 3, 5–6, 17, 18, 19
Standardized achievement
    tests, 8, 20
Standards
  achieving high, 16–17, 20
  assessment for, 22, 27
  setting, 16, 20–22
  state, 72
  support for, 20, 27
  See also NCLB,
        standards/requirements of
*Standards for What? The Economic
    Roots of K-16 Reform,* 156
State role in education, 22, 37–38,
    43, 72–73, 80, 120–122
Steinberg, A, 158
Stern, D., 161
Stigler, James, 101
Stories, importance of, 116–119
Student performance
  by disabled, 3, 45, 70
  by disadvantaged, 3, 7, 45, 127

  by English language learners,
    3, 45, 70
  by minorities, 3, 45, 70
  consequences of poor, 5, 7–8, 19.
        See also NCLB compliance,
        non
  declining, 11
  knowledge and skills, 3
  science and math, 2, 17–19, 28
  short-term, 46
  technology and. *See* Technology
  versus international students,
    2–3, 7–8, 14, 17
  See also Assessment; Evaluation
Study groups, 100–101
Successful schools, characteristics
    of, 20
Superintendents, 109–113, 119
Systems thinking, 57–58

T
Teachers
  accountability of, 121
  as leaders, 30, 104–105, 112, 120,
        123. *See also* Leadership
  collaboration by, 123. *See also*
        Professional development;
        Team work
  culture of, 122
  preparation of, 2–3
  problems of, 6, 15
  professional development for.
        See Professional
        development
  qualifications of, 6, 23–24,
        27, 29–30, 34, 70, 89,
        107, 112–113, 128
  recommendations for/about,
        15, 16, 18
  recruiting/retaining, 21, 122–123
  support for, 44
Team work, 30, 41, 93, 123

Technology
    effects of, 12, 14
    in other countries, 108–109
    Internet, 110
    monitoring student achievement
        with, 72, 76–88, 91
    software, 90, 121
Testing. *See* Adequate yearly
    progress; Assessment
The Expectations Gap, 157
Third International Mathematics
    and Science Study (TIMMS),
    2, 17, 27, 101, 126
Tibbott Elementary School case
    study, 129–147
Time, and learning, 10–12
Title II, 6
Tiwana, Amrit, 32, 67

U
U.S. Department of Education
    abolishment of, 9
    administration of NCLB by, 2,
        22–23, 29, 125
    dissemination of information by,
        4, 22–23
    evaluations, 152–153

policies and practices, 154–158
    research, 98–99, 151–154
    research initiative. *See* What
        Works Clearinghouse
    support from, 28
    Teacher-to-Teacher program, 105
U.S. Secretary of Education, 3
*Uses of Time for Teaching and
    Learning, The,* 12
Using Data to Improve Schools, 38

V
Vallas, Paul, 119
Vocational education, 149, 153–154

W
Welch, Jack, 95–96, 118
What Works Clearinghouse
    (WWC), 28, 52–56, 61–63, 106
Whitehurst, Grover J., 107–108
Whoosh, 119
Wing, J.Y., 161
Wisconsin Center for Education
    Research, 64–65
Working Inside the Black Box, 75
Wright, Wilbur and Orville,
    118–119

**CORWIN
PRESS**

The Corwin Press logo—a raven striding across an open book—represents the union of courage and learning. Corwin Press is committed to improving education for all learners by publishing books and other professional development resources for those serving the field of PreK–12 education. By providing practical, hands-on materials, Corwin Press continues to carry out the promise of its motto: **"Helping Educators Do Their Work Better."**